DI107059

GREECE

A Classical Tour With Extras

GREECE

A Classical Tour With Extras

BY LUCILE & GEORGE BROCKWAY

NEW YORK ▣ ALFRED A KNOPF ▣ 1966

THIS IS A BORZOI BOOK
PUBLISHED BY ALFRED A. KNOPF, INC.

First Edition
© *Copyright 1966 by Lucile and George Brockway*
All rights reserved under International and Pan-American Copyright Conventions. Distributed by Random House, Inc. Published simultaneously in Toronto, Canada, by Random House of Canada Limited.
Library of Congress Catalog Card Number: 66-19371
Manufactured in the United States of America

To Our Children

But of us who must die,
Why should a man sit in darkness
And cherish to no end
An old age without a name,
Letting go all lovely things?

PINDAR, Olympian i

CONTENTS

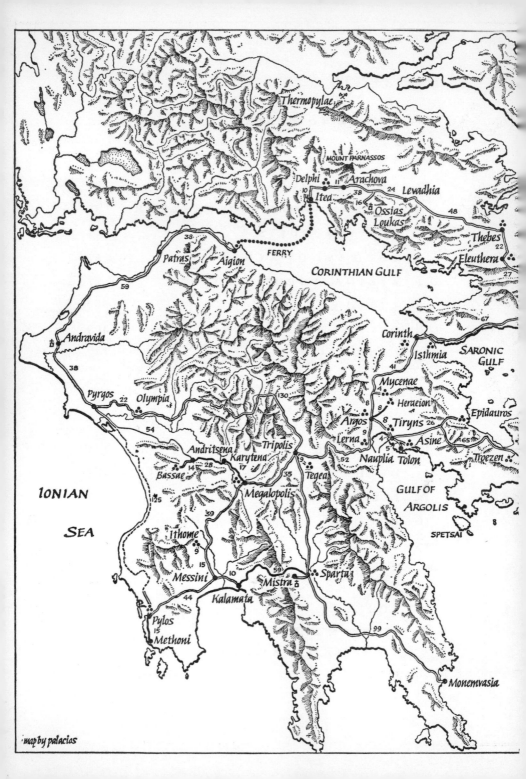

ILLUSTRATIONS

Unless otherwise indicated, all photographs
were taken by George Brockway

following page 48

following page 112

GREECE

A Classical Tour With Extras

A NOTE TO BEGIN

Although the ancients typically had a deep
reverence for the past . . . they displayed
surprisingly little interest in exploring it.
Even the Greeks were generally content
with vague, conflicting, or preposterous leg-
ends. . . . Only the West—the conceited,
irreligious West—has made this pious effort
to know all the cultures and recover the
whole past of mankind.
HERBERT J. MULLER, *The Loom of History*

This is the kind of book we should have liked to
have when we were planning our first trip to Greece—
and are delighted to have now to refresh our memories. It is not an all-inclusive book: no single book—
indeed, no single library—could include everything
worth knowing about Greece. Consequently this is no
substitute for other books but is, rather, a guide to
some of the best of them as well as to the country itself.

It should also be emphasized that this book has a
definite point of view. It does not attempt to be all
things to all people, but those who travel with roughly
the same things in mind as we do will find our pretty
dogmatic advice more useful than the conventional
guide's impersonality.

In a word, our point of view is humanistic. Greece is a ruggedly beautiful land full of immortally beautiful things; yet these do not exist in a vacuum. The leading reason for traveling in Greece is that so much happened there. All philosophy, Whitehead remarked, is a series of footnotes to Plato. Likewise our arts and letters and sciences—our humanities as well as our ways of waging war and organizing peace—all take the forms they do at least in part because of their Greek origins. One travels in Greece, then, in the hope of gaining a better understanding of these origins and hence (more hopefully) a better understanding of ourselves. There is this interest even in the landscape, for a source of wonder to us must be what it meant to the ancient Greeks.

At the same time, it is well to recognize that neither we nor our readers are professionals. Many things that excite archaeologists are to us merely battered stones half buried in the barren earth. The ability to distinguish at sight an amphora by the Pan painter from one by the Diomed painter is a joy we forever renounce. The moves and countermoves of the Peloponnesian War fade all quickly from our minds. Even in the case of the tragedies, which we may read and reread at our leisure, we must follow Ortega in admitting that we do not understand them very well. We are amateurs writing for amateurs.

This need be no handicap for either you or us, for Ancient Greece is our common heritage, which we draw on every day in allusions to Achilles' heel, Pandora's box, the Hippokratic oath, the Oedipus complex. From our childhood on, we have all heard something of Helen of Troy, of the labyrinth and the Minotaur, of the Oracle of Delphi. The Parthenon will not burst upon us as a total surprise, nor will Salamis, nor Parnassos, nor windswept Troy itself.

So we need not be sober-sided about Greece or our trip there. It is, after all, a vacation we have in mind. It is a particular kind of vacation because Greece is the place it is. With so many delights that only Greece can offer, it would be a shame to fritter away time on pleasures that can be enjoyed nearer home. Thus there is little in this book about skin-diving or mountain climbing or nightclubbing, activities which can be pursued in Greece but which no doubt can be enjoyed equally well in places easier to get to. There is very little here about contemporary arts and crafts: plenty of people stand ready to tell you about them on the spot. Nor is there much here about food or drink. The Greeks' successors on the stage of history had it that *de gustibus non est disputandum;* nevertheless, it is not observed that gourmets congregate in Greece.

If we enjoy the mountain air as well as the ruins of Delphi, the plain of Argos as well as the stones of Mycenae, the beaches of Mykonos as well as the mosaics of Delos, we can have the best vacation of our lives.

As we have said, our advice is pretty dogmatic. As

it happens, that there is no law to force you to accept it, but you will at least find it a point of departure.

We tell you about other books to read, some few of which you will want to take with you. These books will cost you time and money (we think you ought to buy copies of your own), but the investment will be a tiny part of your total investment in the trip and will make it much more enjoyable. You will, after all, have so little time in Greece that it would be foolish to waste any part of it finding out for yourself things that others have already found out for you.

We also explain very briefly some general things you need to know that are not—or so we believe—so usefully presented in the other books to which we refer you.

Our purpose, quite simply, is to help you bring it all into focus. A conventional guidebook is indispensable for reference but hopelessly confusing for trip planning; there are too many possibilities, and there seems no way of working even the three-star sights into a feasible itinerary. So we give you an itinerary that has worked for us, and leave to you the problem of fitting in the sights that you are dying to see but we have somehow omitted. You will be surprised how useful this arrangement is. In our own case, we were floundering futilely in trying to plan our first trip until friends gave us the itinerary of their recent excursion. In the end, we scarcely followed in their footsteps at all—they had spent days in places we did not even go to, and vice versa—but their itinerary gave us something to work from. With it in hand, we put our own together in short order. You should be able to use ours in the same way.

We tell you why we make the recommendations we do, but we generally do not attempt detailed descriptions of what you will see; your guidebook will do that. On the other hand, we do give bits of information most guidebooks overlook. For example, at Olympia you will be called on to admire statuary showing a struggle between Lapiths and Centaurs. We tell you who the Lapiths were (subjects of a friend of Theseus') and what inflamed the Centaurs against them (wine and women) and why the Greeks found the story significant (you'll have to read the book to find that out).

Also, from time to time, we quote Homer or Euripides, Herodotos or Thucydides, Pausanias or some other ancient, hoping thereby to add another dimension to the scene before you.

Note: We sometimes give distances in miles and sometimes in kilometers, but not without method. We use kilometers for distances you may be driving, since the odometer of any car you rent in Greece will register kilometers. For distances, you want merely to get an impression of, such as the length of Mount Taygetos, we use miles. Likewise we give prices in drachmas (exchangeable for about 3¢ each) for minor transactions you will be conducting on the spot; for major transactions and for airline tickets and the like, we quote the prices in dollars.

Certain Greek proper names may appear here in a form different from what you have seen in other books. For an explanation of our spelling, see Appendix I, page 243 *f*.

We hope you have as good a time as we have had, and that you remember your vacation in Greece with as much pleasure.

1

THIS IS
OUR PLAN

It is a bad plan that admits of no modification.
PUBLILIUS SYRUS

There is a difference of kind as well as degree between the ruins of Greece and those of the rest of Europe. For the most part, the Greek ruins are really ruins; they are not only not inhabitable, they are scarcely visible. Kenilworth is indeed a ruin, but there is enough left to give one a sense of being in John of Gaunt's great hall, or of following the action of Scott's romance. And in the ruins of Chinon, one can see more or less where Charles VII stood when Joan sought him out. One can also readily see that Kenilworth and Chinon are different kinds of places, and one can compare them, contrast them, and determine their relationships with dozens of similar monuments. But only an archaeologist can make so much out of most of the Greek ruins.

If one does not have Professor Blegen at one's side, Pylos is hard to grasp. And probably the layman does not feel much more in tune with the Mycenaeans for having seen Pylos and Mycenae and Tiryns and Gla instead of merely one of them. Even in the case of later temples, which are in much better condition, the weary or timid traveler may find it difficult to suppress the thought that Bassae is not enough different from the Parthenon or, perhaps, the Hephaesteion to have been worth the rough and worrisome journey to it.

Greece is one place that is better seen by limiting one's sights. We shall therefore recommend that you see the best of each of the various kinds of things Greece has to offer, that you spend enough time with the best to absorb something of their meaning, and that you let the rest go until your next trip. In this way Greece can really be seen in three weeks as England or France or Italy can not.

Our prime recommendations are these:

(1) For the Classic Age at its height: the Athenian Acropolis;

(2) For the glory of all ages and indispensable background: the National Archaeological Museum, Athens;

(3) For the delicacy and the grandeur of Hellenistic and Roman Greece: the Tower of the Winds and the Temple of Olympian Zeus, Athens;

(4) For the beauty of the Archaic Age: Aegina, near Athens;

(5) For the charm of the Byzantine: two or three of the little churches of Athens and the Kaisariani Monastery near Athens;

(6) For the splendor of the Byzantine: the Monastery of Daphne near Athens;

(7) For the seat of the Mysteries: Eleusis, near Athens;

(8) For the seat of Apollonic religion: Delphi;

(9) For an understanding of the power of pedimental sculpture: the Museum of Olympia;

(10) For the might of the Bronze Age: Mycenae and Tiryns;

(11) For a glimpse of the intertwining of scientific medicine, faith healing, and commercialized religion: Epidauros;

(12) For the elegance of the Minoans: Knossos and the Archaeological Museum, Herakleion, Crete;

(13) For remains of the Franks and the Turks: Rhodes;

(14) For what Provincetown wishes it were: Mykonos.

As a benign Providence has surprisingly decreed, these fourteen great places, together with a number of others that can be seen by the way, arrange themselves into three groups, each of which can be pleasantly and profitably seen in about a week. First in importance, of course, is Athens, which, with environs, accounts for the first seven items on our list. The next four items comprise what has come to be known as the Classical Tour. The remaining three offer a glimpse of the islands.

We hasten to admit that many a place you have heard much of does not appear on our list. Corfu and Santorini are not on it. A lover of the Byzantine will shake his head at the omission of Meteora, Mistra, Chios, Mount Athos, Saloniki. A fancier of battles long ago will deplore the absence of Marathon, Thermopylae, Salamis, Plataea. An archaeologist will feel that without Pylos and Dodona and a dozen others one has seen nothing. We have read a delightful book devoted exclusively to the Frankish castles of the Morea (the Peloponnesos, that is), only a couple of which will we even notice in passing. Nor will we pay much attention to sites sacred to the memory of the War of Independence or World War II.

For these and all other omissions we plead one excuse: lack of time. If you have more than three weeks, you can see more. If you want to move a little faster than we recommend, you can work a bit more in. You may, of course, substitute one of your choices for one of ours; but don't blame us if you're disappointed.

Unfortunately, there are so many tourists in Greece in relation to hotel accommodations that you had better plan your itinerary down to the last detail before you start. In order to do this, you will have to get the latest information on boat and plane schedules (for visits to the islands) and on phases of the moon (which are the same as at home).

The first important date is that of the full moon, because the Acropolis of Athens is open to the public for four nights at the time of the full moon (otherwise it closes at sundown). On one of these nights, then, you must be in Athens. Since it is unnecessary—even undesirable—to have your seven days in Athens in a solid block, it should not be too difficult to arrange to be there during the full moon.

Once this date is settled, the rest will fall into place without too much trouble. Ideally, you should spend your first three days in Athens. This will give you time for two trips to the Acropolis and two visits to the National Archaeological Museum, both of which are far too rich to be absorbed at once, and both of which are essential bench marks for what you will subsequently see on your travels. You will also have time for the Temple of Olympian Zeus and the Tower of the Winds and for a daylong expedition. For the latter, we advise a cruise to Aegina.

The next day, other things being equal, you should start off on your Classical Tour. This can be made either clockwise or counterclockwise. Perhaps you should, again, be guided by the phases of the moon, for Delphi, too, should be seen by moonlight if at all possible. Therefore if your Athenian full moon comes during your first stay in Athens, you should take the Classical Tour counterclockwise and head first for Delphi. If, on the other hand, the full moon comes during your second stay, you should take your Classical Tour clockwise, thus leaving Delphi for the last call before your return to Athens.

In either case you will start out on the same road— a road, in fact, that you will traverse again when you go to Daphne and Eleusis. If you like to make early starts (say no later than eight thirty), you can do Daphne and Eleusis on this day and thus have an extra day to use somewhere else; but it would probably be a mistake to push yourself too hard, especially this early in your trip.

At Eleusis the route divides; the clockwise tour continues along the coast to Corinth, while the counter-clockwise one climbs over the eastern flank of Mount Kithairon to Thebes. We shall follow the latter, with the obvious understanding that if you go the other way you will come upon things in the inverse order.

This road will give you your first taste of Greek mountain driving, but it will be more interesting than the new "National Route" (also known as Route No. 1—there is no other numbered route in Greece), which looks like every superhighway you have ever seen. About 50 kilometers from Athens you will come to Eleuthera, one of the most complete ancient systems of fortification, and as such worth a half hour or so of your time (the field of the Battle of Plataea— the last battle of the Persian Wars—is somewhere nearby to the west, but no one knows exactly where). Next you arrive at Thebes, rich in myth and history but with little to see now; however, archaeologists think they know the approximate location of the Palace of Cadmus, which is apparently grander than Mycenae or Knossos, and are trying to get the right to excavate it. Then on to Levadhia, 120 kilometers from Athens, where you should plan to have lunch.*

An enterprising tavernkeeper has set up tables under the trees at the mouth of the gorge. It is green and cool and full of the roar of rushing water. His bill of fare is not extensive; but we happily exercised our few words of Greek and lunched on *psomí* (bread), *féta* (white goat's or sheep's milk cheese), and *bíra* (beer). A few yards above the tavern, an old stone bridge (Frankish or Turkish) carries a path across the stream and up the gorge. If you have brought a picnic (your Athens or Delphi hotel will prepare one if you ask the night before), you will find plenty of places to spread it there.

After lunch, spend a while wandering up the gorge or scrambling up to the Frankish castle that towers above it, but not too long, because Delphi has even more magnificent scenery and much, much more.

* The luncheon spot is not marked and may not be easy to find, even though we shall do our best to direct you; it is worth making the effort, because it is one of the most enchanting places in Greece. Entering town from the direction of Thebes, continue straight ahead, past the road to Delphi (which is to your right). This street will end in a blank wall, at which you should turn right (the only possible way). The next left will take you up an unpromising street to the mouth of the spectacular gorge that contains the ancient springs of Lethe (Forgetfulness) and Mnemosyne (Memory)—no one knows which is which, but it does not matter. Entering town from the direction of Delphi, make a right turn in the center of the town (a left would take you to Thebes), and proceed as above on the street that ends in a blank wall.

If the Byzantine interests you, you should spend a couple of hours at Ossias Loukas, one of the most renowned of monasteries. In any event you should note, where the Ossias Loukas road meets the main highway, that you are now near the crossroads where Oedipus slew his father. Then on to Delphi in plenty of time for dinner. Spend two nights there, and devote all the intervening day and the morning of the following day to exploring Delphi and its museum.

The best hotels in Delphi are the Vouzas at the eastern end of town and the new Amalia and the Hotel des Delphes at the western end. All these are modern and have breathtaking views. The last perhaps has a slight edge, once you discount the Vouzas's dramatic cliffside site, which necessitates entering on the top floor, and taking the elevator *down* to your room. On the other hand, the Vouzas is in a more convenient location for walking to the sanctuary.

In many respects Delphi is a typical tourist trap. It would scarcely be surprising to find shops selling balsam pillows painted "Souvenir of Delphi." Yet neighboring Arachova is famous for woolen goods, particularly shawls and blankets, and Delphi stores have a good selection.

After Delphi, down to Itea (comfortably reached in half an hour; so allow three quarters) to catch the 1:00 p.m. ferry for Aigion.*

* If you are making this tour clockwise, you should leave Olympia by 12:30 to make the 4:00 p.m. ferry at Aigion. Needless to say, you will want to check all these times the night before.

The crossing takes two and half hours. You can buy snacks on the ferry. Then you have an easy drive of roughly 160 kilometers—the only one in Greece without mountains—to arrive in Olympia in time for dinner. On the way, at Andravida, about 100 kilometers from Aigion, you should devote a few minutes to the decaying remains of the Frankish cathedral of Saint Sophia, about a block to the west of the main road near the northern edge of the village.

On the ferry from Itea to Aigion we met an American couple, he of Greek birth and very much older than she. Each of them, on hearing we were bound for Olympia (of course by way of Pyrgos), produced a remark that gave us furiously to think.

Said he: "There's a great thing to see in Pyrgos, but I don't know what it is."

Said she: "There's nothing to do in Olympia if you don't like ruins. There are only two hotels."

We were unable to check on him, but she clearly knew what she was talking about, including her information on the first-class hotels. The newer is the Xenia. Slightly better located because it offers a view of the Altis is the SPAP Hotel (the initials stand for the railroad company that had the foresight to build it). The museum and the Altis are within walking distance of both. The chambermaids and waitresses at the SPAP are charming little black-haired beauties, calling to mind the Minyan maidens of Mary Renault's novels.

Spend two nights, and leave bright and early on the second morning (order a picnic lunch the night before) for Nauplia, about 200 kilometers of mountainous driving away. At Nauplia stay at the Xenia or the Amphitryon: the former is newer and is situated high above the Bay of Argos; the latter is new enough, is located down near the harbor, and has its own swimming pool. Spend three nights, using Nauplia as a base from which to visit Mycenae, Tiryns, Epidauros, Tolon, and Nauplia itself, with possible visits to Troezen, Argos, and Asine and time to relax a bit and swim or sunbathe.

Again make an early morning start; you now return to Athens (about 130 kilometers), visiting Corinth (about 65 kilometers) on the way. Thus endeth the Classical Tour.

You will want to spend two or three days in Athens, seeing things you missed the first time, and particularly doing Daphne and Eleusis, looking up some of the delightful little Athenian Byzantine churches and wandering through the Plaka (the old city—though not old by ordinary European standards). And by all means reserve at least a morning for a return visit to the National Museum, whose exhibits will mean more to you now that you have seen the natural, so to say, habitat of many of them.

Then the islands, Mykonos and Delos; two nights. After a hard week of touring Classical sites, absorbing new information and admiring new wonders every hour, there is no better way to give yourself a change of pace than to take a steamer to Mykonos. Mykonos has become the most famous (and most crowded) vacation spot in Greece. Hardy travelers, or those who have more time to spare, prefer one of the remoter islands. But Mykonos is the jumping-off place for Delos, which you will want to see, and it has its own potent charms, especially if you like people: Greek people, and people of all nationalities, classes and modes of dress and undress. On Mykonos, it's live and let live.

Mykonos's popularity poses some problems with hotel reservations. There are two good hotels on the island, the Leto, on the waterfront, and the new Xenia, a beach-style hotel a little removed from the harbor and hence quieter.* There are two or three other waterfront hotels, more modest than those mentioned, and rooms to be had *chez l'habitant.* Every boat is met by townspeople who have clean rooms to rent, but once in a while there are not enough to go around and youngsters sleep on the beach or in boats drawn up on the shore.

In planning your departure, you should know that there are three ships a week which stop at Mykonos

---

* Debarking and embarking at Mykonos are annoying adventures. No one bothers to tell the traveler what is going on, and the skippers of the harbor lighters only too plainly betray their descent from pirates. If you have reservations at the Xenia and plenty of patience, you may be met by the hotel Microbus—or not impossibly, they may simply forget about your arrival. If so, it is a short walk in the moonlight.

on the way to Rhodes. The alternative is to return to Athens by overnight boat, and when you are ready to go to Rhodes, take the plane. There are two or three flights a day in summer and the fare is moderate (about $17.50).

In Rhodes the Hotel des Roses is first-rate, while the Miramare attracts what *Holiday Magazine* calls the international set (but like the Athens Hilton and the Glyphada Asteria, which have a similar clientele, it is not conveniently located).

Then two nights later, leave for Crete by air. In Herakleion (Crete) the only Class "A" hotel, unfortunately, is the Astir, though the Xenia is a-building.

Two nights there and then back to Athens by air, spend another couple of days taking a last look around, and your three weeks are up. You've had it.

2

HOW AND

HOW MUCH

*The best time for making a voyage is during
the fifty days that follow upon the solstice.*

HESIOD, *Works and Days*

B y far the biggest part of the cost of your vacation
in Greece will be that of getting there and back. The
regular round-trip tourist fare from New York to
Athens (good for one year) is about $750; the 14- to
21-day weekday economy excursion fare is $520 or
$535, depending on the season. Charter flights to Lon-
don, Paris, or Rome, with regular scheduled flights on
to Athens can sometimes be arranged and are very
much cheaper. Unfortunately few of them seem to go
when you want to. Of course, they still run boats; but
New York to Athens takes eleven days via the Greek
Line, and what, then, is left of your vacation?

The only through flights from New York to Athens
are run by Olympic and TWA. We don't know about
Olympic, but we'll never take TWA again, preferring
the inconvenience of changing planes in Amsterdam

(KLM) or Rome (most other lines) to TWA's hectoring huckersterism. When they are not trying to make you look at movies you have no interest in, they are hawking tax-free cigarettes and liquor, so that the aisle is impassable and the hostesses are too busy to get someone to fix a broken seat or otherwise attend to the passengers.

Once you are in Greece, the three practical means of travel, in rising order of convenience and, probably, cost, are bus, private automobile, and yacht.

If you plan to stick to the beaten path, the tour buses can serve you pretty well. Let us say you decide to do the Classical Tour more or less as we describe it in Chapters 8 through 12. A circuit very like this is made by several tours: C.H.A.T. No. 9 and Key Motor Coach Tours No. 12, among others.

The principal trouble with the tours is that they are too fast. Both of those mentioned take only four days, and others do it—Apollo knows how—in two, while we recommend at least a week. The solution is to arrange for stopover privileges. Thus you can roar into Delphi on the bus, jogtrot around the ruins with the tour guide, stay over and prowl around the place at your leisure, and catch another tour on its way through a day or two later. As you will have noticed, there is comparatively little to see between the major places; so even if the bus careens nonstop, you will not miss too much. But without the stopovers, the tour buses can be deadly.

Naturally, a private automobile, whether brought

in, rented, or chauffeur-driven, gives you more freedom of action than does a bus—but not so much as
appears at first glance, principally because hotel reservations are necessary almost everywhere. In Greece
it simply is not possible to ramble without plan
and stop wherever whim dictates—unless you are
equipped for camping or prepared to take potluck
with villagers.

A car is useful for seeing whatever sights you wish
to in Attica and essential for exploring the environs
of Nauplia. Nevertheless, taxis are available at both
places for roughly $20 a day.

There remains the possibility of a yacht. Don't
smile. In some circumstances it may be both the best
and the cheapest of all.

Consider first the fact that the ancient Greeks themselves often found the sea the safest and surest means
of travel about their rugged land. Most of the places
you will want to visit, therefore, are close to the sea.
Consider second the fact that you will have to have
shelter no matter how you travel: this is included in
the yacht hire, which can work out to less than $20
a day a person, though of course it will run much
higher if you travel in style.

There are, on the other hand, three conditions that
have to be met. First, you must be able to put together
a party of six or more congenial people, unless either
expense or comfort is no object. Second, you need
somewhat more time, because you will not often travel
at night and your yacht is not likely to cruise at more

than ten knots. Third, you need a reliable and knowledgeable agent to arrange things, because it is possible to be taken for a sleigh ride instead of a cruise. We strongly recommend Captain Timoleon Louys, Delmouzos & Louys, 4 Kriezotou Street, Athens 134.

It is worth thinking about. To help your thinking, here is a possible itinerary for a yachting cruise in lieu of the Classical Tour on land:

1st day: Leave Piraeus; visit Aegina, Troezen, and possibly Hydra; overnight at Nauplia.

2nd day: Visit Mycenae, Tiryns, and possibly Argos; overnight at Nauplia.

3rd day: Visit Epidauros, Palamedi, and Asine; overnight at Tolon.

4th day: Sail to Monemvasia; visit and overnight.*

5th day: Sail early for Pylos (this is an all-day cruise; it would be possible to sail instead to Gytheion and from there visit Sparta and Mistra, thus adding a day to the itinerary; but as we say elsewhere, we recommend visiting Mistra extensively or not at all); overnight at Pylos.

6th day: Visit Nestor's palace, Sphacteria Island, and possibly Methoni; overnight cruise to Katakalon.

7th day: Visit Olympia; overnight at Katakalon.

8th day: Sail to Naupaktos (site of Battle of Lepanto, 1571); overnight.

* It is a pity that it is really not practical to work Monemvasia into a short land itinerary, for it is an imposing Frankish-Byzantine remain.

9th day: Sail to Itea; visit Delphi; overnight at Itea.

10th day: Visit Delphi; overnight at Itea.

11th day: Sail to Corinth; sail to Loutraki for overnight.

12th day: Sail to Eleusis; sail to Piraeus; finis.

This cruise takes longer than the land journey, but not so much as it seems at first, because the cruise includes places that otherwise would probably be done from Athens. When allowance is made for these (Aegina and Eleusis), the difference in elapsed time is only three days; and the cruise has provided, by way of bonus, visits to Monemvasia, Pylos, Loutraki, and for what it is worth, Lepanto, together with whatever pleasures may be derived from traveling by yacht. And if you are not, at the end of eleven days, sick of the pleasures of yachting, you might skip Eleusis and proceed out through the Saronic Gulf to Mykonos, Delos, and as many other of the Cyclades as you have the time or inclination for.

Travel agents can save you a good bit of time and trouble, particularly if you use an agent who lives in Greece to make your arrangements for that country. April and May reservations can be made as late as February (though summer reservations should be made *earlier*). Nevertheless you must be able to try Hotel X quickly when Hotel Y proves to be full. Obviously this sort of thing can be done better on the scene in Greek than by airmail in English.

We highly recommend John Spyrakis, 6 Bucharest

Street, Athens 133, who has been in the business for years and has endorsements from people like the late Edith Hamilton, Sir Laurence Olivier, and us. His only fault is that he may want to do too much for you; if you don't want to be coddled, let him know and he will oblige.

On the other hand, he or one of his young men will, if you wish, act as your driver and guide you throughout the whole trip, or meet you at the airport and whisk your bags through customs, or plan your itinerary, or simply make your reservations. We planned our itinerary from our reading and the reports of friends (just as you are doing now), but we made many changes at Mr. Spyrakis's suggestion and were generally glad we did.

It is possible to get around very cheaply in Greece traveling by local bus or hitchhiking, staying in Youth Hostels or rooms rented from the locals, or camping out. Thousands of youngsters from all over the world do this every year. We had enjoyable times with two hitchhikers—Siwart, a young Dutchman we picked up (or were picked up by) first on the Aigion Ferry, again at Sparta, and finally at Epidauros; and Finn, a Dane we met first at Kalamata, later at Tolon, and last in Istanbul.

The National Tourist Police can be a great help in finding rooms, making phone calls, and giving all sorts of advice. Don't hesitate to use them. They are identified by an armband displaying the flag of the country whose language they speak. Each Tourist Policeman speaks at least one foreign language, though it may not be English.

We assume that most of our readers have reached the age when vagabonding has been left behind and therefore our recommendations will usually be first-class hotels, with comfort, but not luxury, in mind. There are all sorts of in-between hotels. To cope with the flow of tourists the Greek government has sponsored the building of a number of new tourist hotels throughout the country, each one called Xenia, after the Greek word for stranger or guest. They are generally attractive and comfortable.

The Greek system of classifying hotels makes no sense to anyone except (possibly) a Greek hotel-keeper. A hotel that may once have been accorded an "A" rating because it was the first in its neighborhood to have water laid on still retains the rating, regardless of the present state of its accommodations. A brand-new Xenia, like that on Mykonos, which gives you sitting room, bedroom, bath, and balcony for about $5 a night, for two, is classified "B." If you plan to stray from the path we have beaten for you, and if you want to try your hand at getting your own reservations,* you should pick up a copy of *Greece on $5*

---

* Self-arranged reservations can have surprising results. Friends of ours read in one of the travel sections of a new Xenia beach hotel south of Kalamata. It sounded like a pleasant break in a couple of weeks of serious sight-seeing; so they wrote for reservations, which were duly confirmed. They approached Kalamata from Sparta, finishing the difficult drive over Taygetos in the

a Day (Pocket Books, $1.95), which gives details on all hotels, except most of the relatively expensive ones we recommend. It adopts a rather belligerent mucker pose on matters of history, archaeology, and art, but is a convenient source for a lot of practical information—bus lines, boat schedules, restaurant prices, and the like.

One caveat to proud possessors of bad backs; even relatively modern places like the above-mentioned Mykonos Xenia often have sadly sagging springs. If you need a bed board, take a folding one with you.

It is possible, through judicious use of Olympic Airways, to see a good deal of Greece that would otherwise be inaccessible to the ordinary vacationer. Working clockwise, one can do Kalamata in the southern Peloponnesos, Kerkira (Corfu), Agrinion and Ioannina, Larissa and Kozani, Thessaloniki, Kavala, Alexandroupolis, Limnos, Istanbul (Turkey), Mytilene (Lesbos), Izmir (Turkey), Samos, Kos, and as we have already seen, Rhodes and Crete. The trouble is that, with the exception of the Rhodes-Crete connection, there is no airplane service from one of these outposts to another. Each has to be taken by itself, on its merits, at the expense of at least two days and, given the relatively thin schedules, generally three or four.

---

early evening, and took the only road south in eager anticipation of a swim, cocktails, and dinner. They never found the hotel, for the simple reason that it had not yet been built.

Consequently these jaunts are not to be taken lightly, especially if one is timid about bouncing around in old DC-3's or DC-4's. We ourselves have made only one of these possible excursions, though we have seen most of the objectives by land or sea. Unless you have compelling special interests, these are best left off your first-trip itinerary.

We have had scant experience with organized cruises and have no desire for more. It is not that we object to having someone plan our itinerary for us, or arrange our reservations, or handle the baggage and tips and whatnot. There is no virtue that we can see in wrestling with these things on your own; you don't have to go a quarter of the way around the world to worry about getting your baggage off from or on to a plane.

The trouble with cruises is the people on them. And that is not quite what we mean either, because generally they are decent enough, like most people. But cruise people too often are on cruises because they can't think of anything else to do. The travel folders are attractive, and so off they go. But they are really not interested in history or art or even current affairs; their pleasures are sunbathing and shopping. The cruise directors do their best to satisfy the majority— and thus dissatisfy sober souls like ourselves.

In her wonderfully amusing *Europe Without George*, Irene Kampen describes the arrival of a cruise at Delos: "When we reached land we tiptoed across the sandy beach, awed into silence by the island's almost palpable aura of vanished glory. Suddenly a throng of Greeks appeared around the corner of a ruin and began to sell embroidered pocketbooks, gift aprons, and Kodak Instamatic film. Most of the passengers, crazed by an entire day out of touch with the marts and bazaars of Athens, started to buy everything in sight and could hardly be torn away by the tour director to go see the Portico of the Bulls."

Our one cruise was on the Typaldos Lines' *Kriti*— an unattractive old bucket, now in the interisland service, that we cannot recommend for any purpose, and certainly not for her "Lucullan Dinning Room" (*sic*). We took her, however, because we wanted to get to Troy, and she seemed the most convenient way at the time. When we arrived at Chanakale (Çanakkale), the woebegone Turkish village that is Troy's port, it turned out that only about forty of the two hundred on the cruise wanted to take the twenty-mile bus trip to Troy. Really! Then when we got to the ruins it began to drizzle (we are rainmakers and could, we are sure, conjure up a downpour on the Sahara). So the forty of us set off around the well-marked ruins at a smart pace that became smarter as the rain became heavier. We did the whole thing in half an hour and then ducked into the little museum there to wait for the rain to stop, which it did in another half hour. Thirty-six of the forty thereupon joyfully reboarded the buses. Only one British couple and ourselves wanted to go back and do Troy right. "We'll probably never in our lives get back here again," the British lady protested. But in vain. Back to the ship we went.

And that is why we don't like cruises.*

Possible exceptions to the general run of cruises are those of the Hellenic Travellers Club. Lectures on shipboard and at the sites are given by distinguished British scholars and hearty retired vicars who, like Fielding's Parson Adams, have long solaced them-selves with Aeschylus in the original. A botanist and a professional bird watcher are also usually part of the staff. This may all sound frightfully earnest, but friends of ours who have been along are enthusiastic supporters. The cruises are generally oversubscribed; and to be reasonably sure of getting on the one you want, you must join the Club. Overseas membership costs all of ten shillings six pence ($1.47) a head. Address the Assistant Secretary, Hellenic Travellers Club, 11–13 Ridgmount Street, London, W. C. 1. Fares run from about $350 to about $1,000 (plus "wines, spirits, and laundry") from London to London for sixteen-day cruises.

Now that Troy has come up, we might as well say that you had better know your *Iliad* cold if you expect

---

* Lest, by the way, you masochistically leap to the conclusion that this is the sort of thing one must expect with Americans, we should point out that Americans were in a minority on this cruise, being outnumbered by both Germans and British. Cruise people are international.

to get much from it. If you do make the trip—and there are better means than the Typaldos Lines for doing it—be sure to spend some time in the museum in Chanakale. It has some austerely and delicately beautiful golden wreaths or diadems, the like of which we have seen nowhere else. Unluckily, we had no flashbulbs with us; so we cannot show you.

And now that Turkey has come up, we will say only this much more. Most cruises go to Ephesos, but not Pergamon. A pity. Pergamon is by far the more interesting and beautiful site, or sight. We saw it in a thunderstorm, naturally, and it is high on our list of places to go back to. Pergamon is worth an effort, but probably on your second trip. There is a lot to see in Turkey.

3

ATHENS:
FOOD AND SHELTER

Of all the unchristian beverages that ever
passed my lips, Turkish coffee is the worst.
MARK TWAIN, *The Innocents Abroad*

The hotels of Athens have their problems. At any given moment their desk clerks, their cashiers, their porters, and their telephone operators are trying to pacify, enlighten, or simply do routine business with a half dozen more or less bothered customers in three or four different tongues, none of them Greek. A certain amount of confusion results: that much of it the Greeks understand and enjoy.

We have stayed at three different Athenian hotels and have visited friends at a couple of others. Of these five, we rank the Amalia first, largely because its confusion is minimal. Its rooms are on the small side, have only one easy chair to a double room, and are beginning to look shabby. But it shares these features with all its rivals except the Hilton (of which more later).

A few further points might be made:

First, a general caveat: most Athens hotels advertise that they are air-conditioned. This may mean that the manager has an out-of-order window unit in his private office; it certainly cannot be counted on to mean that the guests' rooms are air-conditioned. "Fully air-conditioned" is perhaps more likely to mean what it says. But if you want an air-conditioned room (and from mid-June to mid-September you probably do), you will be well advised to say so specifically when writing for reservations (it will be charged for separately on your bill). The same goes for the cruise ships.

Second, Athens is one of the noisiest cities on earth; the traffic is voluminous, incessant, and roaring. If you are not used to this sort of thing, you should go to the Grande Bretagne and ask for a room on an interior court. This will entail the sacrifice of the partially blocked view of the Parthenon that you might otherwise get by craning your neck out the window of some other room, but it may enable you to get some sleep. Of course, if you don't mind the noise you will find a balcony room (most new hotels have balconies) a delightful place to have breakfast, or just to sit and look.

Third, regardless of what your travel agent may say, pass up the Hilton. Even if there were not other things against it (and there are), its location would rule it out. In a city like Athens you want to be able to wander about the streets in the cool of the evening (when shops are open), and also to duck back into your hotel in the heat of the day (when everything is closed for the siesta). If you stayed at the Hilton, a taxi ride would have to precede and succeed your wandering. Taxis aren't particularly expensive (15 drachmas will get you almost anywhere) but they do take the edge off wandering.

So your choice should be narrowed down to the hotels within hailing distance of Constitution Square (Syntagma Square). Some would have you believe that the location will stamp you as a tourist; if you can fool anyone into thinking you are anything else, you have no need of this book. At the moment, next to the Amalia, the best hotels are probably the Grande Bretagne, the King George, and the Athénée Palace, but new ones are being built all the time.

We have forced ourselves to appear to recommend an Athenian hotel, but what can we say about restaurants? Not much. Yet you must eat. One night you should eat at the King George's top-floor restaurant for the view of the floodlit Acropolis. Also with a good nocturnal view of the Acropolis is the Dionysos, a modish and rather expensive restaurant, which appears on some maps as a Tourist Pavilion across the street from the driveway that leads up to the Acropolis. Bear in mind that the Acropolis is not lighted on those moonlit nights when it is open to the public. One night you should eat at the Taverna tou Vlakhou, merely because it is expected of serious tourists and has a view. Once or twice you might try Ta Kalamia in a courtyard at 5 Stadiou Street, which is authentically Greek and fairly pleasant in a slovenly way. For the rest, you might as well eat in your hotel, or at Zonar's or Floka's, international-type cafés and restaurants.

You may hear elsewhere of Costi's and the Vrahos, but you will not hear of them from us. The former embodies all the delights of a run-down boarding-house in a second-class English resort (rather like *Separate Tables*); the latter is regularly taken over by tours and cruises doing Athens-By-Night.

If it is your curious ambition to re-enact a scene or two from *Never On Sunday*, you were born too late. By the time this book appears, the Greeks will have been driven from virtually all the tavernas in Athens and most of those in Piraeus as well. A Greek friend took us to one that only recently had seemed "typical" and we arrived to discover three quarters of it laid out in long tables radiating from a minuscule dance floor and reserved for one of the tours. The level of entertainment was fully equal to that of a roadhouse in Scranton, Pennsylvania, on a Saturday night. The food did not quite reach that standard, but the cost thereof handsomely exceeded it.

It should perhaps be remarked parenthetically (if at all) that the modern Greek sex symbol on display was, like (dare we say it?) her ancient predecessor the Aphrodite of Melos, rather thick waisted and heavy thighed for our calorie-conscious taste. She did, however, climb, good-naturedly but a trifle ponderously, onto the tour tables and while sashaying to the strains of an electric *bouzouki*, kiss the fortunately bald gentlemen on the pate. They responded according to the dictates of their national conscience: the British with the stiff upper lip and wan smile of the good sport shouldering the waning burden of empire; the Americans in their best pseudo-British manner; the Germans self-consciously on the boisterous side; and the puritanical French in prim silence.

While there is little about Greek food likely to please many visitors, there are two Greek drinks calculated to shock them profoundly—coffee and retsina.

Of course, no experienced American expects to find a decent cup of coffee east of Sandy Hook. Even so, one is surprised and, indeed, hurt the first time one orders American coffee and is served a cup of warm (certainly not hot) water, a communal tin of Nescafé, and a spoon. What the Greeks call French coffee comes somewhat closer to what we are used to.

Turkish coffee is something else again. Mark Twain says: "The cup is small, it is smeared with grounds; the coffee is black, thick, unsavory of smell and execrable in taste." Like most of Mark Twain, this is the truth, mainly. Yet Turkish coffee need not be offensive if one resolutely refuses to think of it as coffee (and needless to say, avoids it at breakfast). It doesn't look, taste, or smell like coffee and so may be imbibed (sparingly, to be sure) as some quite new and different and more or less tolerable beverage, literally a new taste sensation.

The other troublesome beverage is *retsina* (resinated wine), for which it is said to be possible to develop a taste. Perhaps. In any case, there is an acceptable, inexpensive, and non-resinated *vin ordinaire* that goes by the trade name of Demestica and is available white, red or *rosé*.

Coffee brings to mind breakfast, which you will usually take in your room throughout Greece. If, as happens in many instances, there is no telephone in your room, remember to place your order the night before. You can get practically anything you want (except good coffee). The orange juice will generally be fresh and excellent. Mount Hymettos honey has been famous since Classical times. Considering what you are likely to get to eat later, you will be well advised to make breakfast the best meal of your day.

4

THE ACROPOLIS

(*O to be a metope*
now that triglyph's here)
E. E. CUMMINGS, *Is* 5

The Acropolis of Athens is one of the great places of the world. You will want to go back again and again. See it all once, go away to think about it, and then return at every off moment you have, including if possible, once by moonlight. You may never see another thing so wonderful in all your life. Make the most of it and read what your guidebook has to say about it even before you start your trip.

Because you are really going to read that guidebook, we shall confine ourselves to a few points that may not be conveniently covered in it. First, a few words about the Doric temple, of which the Parthenon is the prime example.

We all learned at our mother's knee that the floor (stylobate, if you want to be fancy about it), columns, and various other parts of a Greek temple that appear

47

to be straight are actually subtly curved so that they will seem to be straight. This astonishing commonplace was first measured by a gentleman by the name of Pennethorne in 1837 and has formed the principal topic of guides' conversation ever since. If you want to know more about it, look up *entasis* in the dictionary, because we think that all that matters is that there is some and we do not propose to mention it again.

It is possible to argue that a great architecture emerges when originally unrelated elements prove to work together harmoniously, or when an aesthetic value is developed in a structural member. In this sense "form follows function" has meaning. An example might be Gothic flying buttresses: the most daring structurally tend also to be the most satisfying aesthetically.

A more striking example is found in the Doric temple. Consider the triglyphs and the metopes. The triglyphs are the blocks carved with two plain vertical grooves (leaving three glyphs in relief) that appear above every column and between every pair of columns. The metopes are the more or less square blocks, generally carved with mythical scenes, that appear between each pair of triglyphs.

Triglyphs are thought to be hangovers from the days when temples were built of wood: they were the butt-ends of the massive roof or ceiling beams and, as such, provided a rhythmical decoration of

ATHENS *The Acropolis from the Pnyx*

ATHENS   *The Erechtheion (facing); The Parthenon—detail showing relative spacing of columns (above); The Temple of Olympian Zeus (below)*

SOUNION   *The Temple of Poseidon*

AEGINA   *The Temple of Aphaia, showing second story*

IV

ATHENS   *The Hephaesteion*

BASSAE   *The Temple of Apollo*

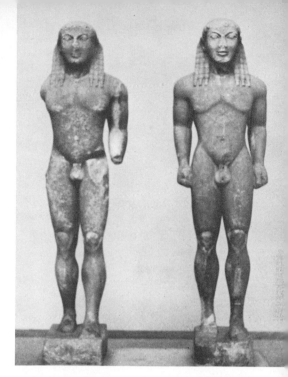

BRAURON *Stoa of the Sanctuary of Artemis (facing, top)*

ELEUSIS *The propylaea and, in the background, the entrance to Hell (facing, bottom)*

DELPHI *Kleobis and Biton, Delphi Museum (right); The Tholos (below)*

VII

DAPHNE *A mural of St. Gregory in the south aisle*

ATHENS *The Church of the Kapnikarea*

no special moment. The spaces between them, then as later, offered opportunities for carving or painting. When, however, the temple received a peristyle (that is, columns all around), problems appeared in the corners. If the triglyph over the end column is centered directly above it (as are all the others), then the end metope is a poor thing, less than a third the size of the others. A sculptor cannot do much with it, because corner metopes force his reliefs to turn the corner and he cannot think of a satisfactory way to do that. Besides, in contrast with the heavily accented triglyphs, a small corner metope makes the corner of the building seem to hang in the air.

At first glance the solution is easy enough: eliminate the end metope by putting the end triglyph at the very corner instead of over the center of the end column. The eye still follows the flutings of the column to those of the triglyph, and all is well. Except. Except that the metope next to it now becomes sensibly larger than the others.

So the only thing is to fudge a little. Hold the metopes equal in size, but bring the end column in a little and make it and its triglyph a little heavier than their neighbors and perhaps the differences will not be noticed.

Very well.

At the same time there is trouble with the peristyle. The corner columns are generally seen without a background; all the others have the rest of the building behind them. As a result, the corner columns seem lighter than the others and thus the corner of the building seems to hang in the air.

Again the solution is to fudge a little. Make the corner columns a little heavier than the others and bring them in a little closer to their neighbors.

But this solution is the same as that for the problem of the metopes. It is miraculous. And so (meaning consequently) is the Doric temple.

Of course, this is not the only possible solution. Some temples, notably one at Paestum in Italy, keep the end triglyphs centered over the end columns and stop the entablature (lintel) right there, thus forcing the column capitals considerably beyond the roof line. This extreme was not widely adopted.

In the Parthenon, on the other hand, the notion of thickening the corner columns and bringing them closer to their neighbors so recommended itself to the architects that the end metopes had to be made *narrower* than the others.

Thus the Doric temples are various, though their variety is much less than that of almost any other style. And this is striking in view of the absence of central organization in Greek religion. It almost seems as though the architectural style plays the role that elsewhere is played by an ecclesiastical hierarchy and sacred books.

An interesting feature of the Parthenon, and indeed of most Greek temples, is the relatively small room at the western end of the building. This room, which had no entrance to the sanctuary, was used to store trophies and the spoils of war. It became, in fact, a sort of state treasury, with both a large and a small "t." It is not impossible that it lent gold to private citizens for suitable purposes.

The conjunction of treasury and shrine—which we shall see in different form in Delphi and Olympia— demonstrates that the Greek religion was established. It also demonstrates the power of the gods, for enormous wealth could be safely stored in sacred precincts, and only there.

The Parthenon is such a large and majestic building that it comes as a surprise to realize that inside it was dark and crowded. Indeed, all Greek temples were dark and crowded inside, for the Greeks had scarcely begun to learn the uses of space. Or perhaps it should be said that they had no particular use for interior space, because no services were held inside the temples. The altars were outside, in the open air, generally in front of the temple's east front, although there were many altars scattered around without relation to temples. Considering the amount of fat that was burnt on the altars, one can understand why they could not be indoors.

So the temples were merely places to keep things, mainly the cult statue, but also the cult, or state, treasure. None of the cult statues has survived and authorities do not agree about their size (which is in point here). What is perhaps more surprising is the fact that the disagreeing authorities serenely disdain to even mention that there is difference of opinion. Apparently meticulous plans of the Parthenon are given on page 24 of Richter's *A Handbook of Greek Art* and on page 375 of Berve and Gruben's *Greek Temples, Theaters and Shrines.* The former (though no scale is presented with the drawing) shows the base of Athena's statue as about 26 feet by 13 feet; the latter about 24 by 8 feet. Not even the proportions are the same. Dinsmoor's *The Architecture of Ancient Greece* (page 164) gives the dimensions as 26 feet 4½ inches by 13 feet 5¼ inches. This is a question of fact, not an opinion poll; Dinsmoor was there with a tape measure.

In any case, the statues were, according to our taste, extraordinarily large in relation to the space available. The narrowness of that space is difficult to appreciate from the ruins, which lead us to imagine the interior as wide as the exterior. Of course it wasn't. More than a quarter of the exterior width is devoted to the peristyle. The interior colonnade and the walls take up as much more, so that only about a quarter of the width of the building is left unencumbered inside. In the case of the Parthenon, this space is about 30 feet wide, which is not inconsiderable except when filled with a statue whose base leaves only 2 or 3 feet on either side.

Smaller temples were, of course, correspondingly

more cramped, as the Hephaesteion shows, even without its interior colonnade.

A word about color. The mother who told us about *entasis* told us also that the Greeks painted their temples. But not gaudily. The columns, the architrave, the walls, the steps remained white: clean stone where marble was used, marble stucco over limestone or tufa elsewhere. The frieze and the carved metopes were accentuated with blue or black backgrounds. The grooves of the triglyphs were also black. The soffit of the cornice was red.

We have said nothing about the other wonders of the Acropolis: the Propylaea (*pro* means "forward"; *pylae* means "gates"), the Nike Temple, the Erechtheion, the various Pelasgian or Mycenaean remains. You must see them for yourself. Incidentally, you will find to your surprise—at least, we were surprised—that the Porch of the Maidens is really a thing of beauty. No picture does it justice. You will also find that the details of the Erechtheion's columns are exquisite.

From the Belvedere at the eastern end of the Acropolis one has a view of the heights of the Attic hinterland: from left to right, Parnes, Pentelikon, Hymettos. In the foreground is the astonishing high knob of Lykabettos, which, in a military sense, seems to dominate the Acropolis. Why, one wonders, did the ancient Athenians leave it unoccupied and, moreover, outside the walls? And why did the Spartans fail to seize it and end the Peloponnesian War in one blow? Slowly the answer dawns: in ancient times Lykabettos had no military value. It lacked water; so it could not withstand a siege. And it was too far away from the Acropolis or anything else to serve as a platform for hurling any missile within the capabilities of Greek technology. Now it might be different.

The hills at the western end of the Acropolis were within the city walls. The Hill of the Muses at the left, crowned since A.D. 114 by the Philopappos Monument, was fortified in 322 B.C.

Next comes the Pnyx, where the Athenian Assembly met to decide affairs of state and where one now can sit and watch the Sound and Light show. And on the right is the Areopagos, or Hill of Ares. Here the citizens sat as a court of law. Here Orestes was acquitted, Themistokles (so recently a hero on the Pnyx and at Salamis) banished, and Sokrates condemned. Scant trace of these events can be found on the bare rocks.

Against the southern flank of the Acropolis are the Theater of Dionysios and the Odeon of Herodes Atticus. The Theater of Dionysios is built on the site of the theater where the works of the great Athenian dramatists were first performed—but they were not performed in the present theater. In fact, we have no theater dating from the time of the existing plays, nor any play dating from the time of the existing theaters. This has been a boon to scholars interested in disputing how Aeschylus staged *Agamemnon*. To-day the ancient plays are given in the refurbished Odeon.

Odeon means, roughly, "lecture hall"; and one theory has it that Herodes Atticus built his Odeon because he liked to hear himself talk and thought his fellow citizens should not be denied the same pleasure. He was, actually, famous among his contemporaries as a rhetorician and scholar, though no work certainly his has come down to us.

The name of Herodes Atticus will keep cropping up as we make the Classical Tour: he was *there*, sometime between his birth in A.D. 101 and his death in 177. His career illustrates how cosmopolitan was the Roman Empire of his day. He was born near Marathon in Attica of a wealthy family, was appointed praefect of the Free Towns of Asia by Hadrian and subsequently was elected archon in Athens and then became consul in Rome, largely because of his part in the education of Marcus Aurelius and Lucius Verus.

He was a great builder or refurbisher of public buildings: not only the Odeon in Athens but also the Stadium; in Delphi, the Stadium; springs and fountains in Olympia, Corinth, and Thermopylae. In spite of all this, he apparently was unpopular. Sharp business dealings on the part of his father are said to have blackened the family name.

Herodes Atticus' works suggest a lesson for today. He built what would now be called living memorials.

Almost all were useful. Nary a temple, nary a triumphal arch, nary an altar, though Pausanias mentions four golden horses with ivory hooves in the Temple of Poseidon at the Isthmus. Scholars know to whom they were dedicated (generally his wife), but they are all known by *his* name. Is this not the fate—perhaps the intended fate—of living memorials? They are built for the use of the living; they turn out to immortalize their builders: let the honored dead remember themselves.

5

THE REST
OF ATHENS

Of old are Erectheus' folk favored of heaven.
EURIPIDES, *Medea*

Athens is full of museums, two of which are obligatory: the Acropolis Museum and the National Archaeological Museum. You cannot see Greece without seeing both, and you must allow at least one full day (perhaps broken up into several sessions a couple of hours long) for the latter.* In both museums you will want a guide or a detailed guidebook such as Hachette's.

The National Museum at once seizes you by placing just inside the center door the golden death mask of Agamemnon, so called by Schliemann, who may, after all, have been right. Agamemnon or not, the man was kingly, and it is proper to start with him. Your awe will grow as you proceed, and you will be

* Neither museum is open at all hours or every day; better check at your hotel.

grateful for whatever preparatory reading you have done.

We could scarcely begin even to list all the wonders to be seen, and will mention here only one of them, because to us it is the greatest statue ever made: the bronze Zeus of the Thunderbolt. He stands with his right arm poised to hurl the thunderbolt (some say he is Poseidon about to throw his trident), his left arm outstretched for balance. It is not by his size (he is slightly over life-size), but by the perfection of his form and the majesty and tenderness of his expression that we know he is a god. Here is the human figure made divine.

This incomparable statue was discovered by chance by some fishermen off Cape Artemision in 1929. It had lain under the sea for over two thousand years, probably lost when it was being transported to the east. Other bronzes have recently been found in the sea or under the earth. Bronze was too valuable a metal to survive as statuary, except when hidden.

To the right of the entrance to the National Museum is a door with an inconspicuous sign announcing plaster reproductions for sale. We will let you in on a mystery that it took us two years to penetrate (guards at the museum are evidently sworn not to tell): the salesroom is open only in the morning. It is worth a visit. It has scores—perhaps hundreds—of reproductions of all sizes and periods. Unfortunately they are frankly plaster and so do not approach the verisimilitude of the imitation stone reproductions of Alva Museum Replicas, Inc., sold by Brentano's in New York. On the other hand, Alva has only things from the Louvre.

There is another drawback—the museum will not pack or ship its wares for you. So if your fancy lights on an Olympian Apollo or even a Kritios Boy, you will have an awkward companion on your flight home. We have satisfied ourselves with copies of the Cycladic aulos player and a terra-cotta Tanagra woman with pointed hat and veil. The former cost 150 drachmas, the latter 80. They have many others of this size (8 to 10 inches high) and price range, but for some reason nothing Mycenaean. Originals, by the way, of whatever size or degree, can be exported only with a special license; in practice this means they cannot be exported.

The Acropolis Museum is very much smaller but will occupy an afternoon or more. Of particular and curious interest is its large collection of *kouroi* (youths) and *korai* (maidens). *Kore* (the singular of *korai*) was another name for Persephone, whose abduction by Hades and salvation by Demeter were the heart of the Eleusinian mysteries. The *korai* in the Acropolis Museum were connected with Persephone, for they carry her symbol, the pomegranate. But they were also generalized maidens who were placed in the Parthenon to guard and tend the cult treasure. This function had once been performed by living girls, but the stone ones probably served about as well.

There is one more curious thing about these *korai:*

they were all buried, more or less carefully. Indeed, much of what is on display in the Acropolis Museum was similarly accorded burial, for this was the Greek practice with sanctified statuary that had, for one reason or another, outlived its usefulness. A modern parallel might be the procedure for the destruction of worn-out flags. A worn-out flag may not be used as a cleaning rag, and an out-of-style *kore* could not be broken up for lime.

One of the statues found thus buried on the Acropolis is the so-called Kritios Boy, a beautiful youth carved in Parian marble around 480 B.C. The statue is small, only 2 feet 10 inches high. Here the old stiffness has gone; there is still vigor and, for the first time, the grace of the great Classical period that was soon to come.

A large room in the right wing of the Acropolis Museum contains fragments of the frieze of the balustrade of the Temple of Nike, especially that lovely lady fastening her sandal, and four panels from the east frieze of the Parthenon depicting the Panathenaic Procession—not much compared to what is in the British Museum and the Louvre, but enough to make this room memorable.

THE AGORA, HEPHAESTEION, AND KERAMEIKOS

The Agora, or ancient marketplace and civic center, lies spread out to view below and to the north of the

Acropolis. It is a large field with a jumble of very
ruined ruins, carefully excavated and studied by the
American School of Classical Studies, which also rebuilt the Stoa of Attalos at great expense, through
the largesse of American philanthropists. The stark
whiteness and newness of this long colonnaded building offends some sensibilities, mostly British. Foreign
comments on the museum installed in the Stoa always
include the word "didactic" ("a Greek remark!") used
in a slightly derogatory sense. We suspect sour grapes.
The Agora Museum is fascinating, at least to Americans, who are so naïve as to like to learn. The exhibits include a machine used for choosing jurors by lot;
some *ostraka*, the pottery chips used in voting to
ostracize a man; a tribute list, showing how much
each member state paid into the Athenian Confederation; and certainly interesting, even if macabre,
a child's skeleton completely covered with gold leaf.

As a building the Stoa is interesting, too, with its
long covered walkway onto which the shops open—
a perfect adaptation of architecture to climate and
purpose. Here many a bargain was struck and many
a tall tale told by what we would call cracker-barrel
philosophers, as well as by those philosophers better
known to history.

An hour here will suffice for the most avid learners
and then you can wander in the Agora over toward
the Hephaesteion. Forget the guidebooks and what
stones are the remains of what buildings. Just pick

the poppies, which grow in profusion in the heart of this city, a nation's capital.

The Hephaesteion (which used to be called the Theseion until scholars decided it was dedicated to Hephaestos, the god of all smiths and Smiths) is the best preserved of all Greek temples, but it is not very interesting, perhaps for that reason. As Koko says to Katisha:

> *"There's a fascination frantic*
> *In a ruin that's romantic;*
> *Do you think you are sufficiently decayed?"*

It was made into a Christian church early on, which explains the barrel-vaulted ceiling. Many of the metopes still bear finely carved renderings of the exploits of Theseus and Herakles. The shrubbery surrounding the temple is the work of the American School, which reconstructed the third-century landscaping from the planting holes found there. All the shrubs are labeled, to the delight of amateur botanists and those of us who would otherwise not know an oleander from a pomegranate tree, a myrtle from a laurel. There can be few more pleasant places to rest your feet than the garden beside this temple.

Beyond the Hephaesteion lie the Dipylon Gate and the Sacred Gate, where the great Panathenaic Processions started; and beyond the gates the ancient cemetery called the Kerameikos, obviously the same word as "ceramics." This is the original potter's field, or

we'll eat our hats, though of course Judas' silver was
used to buy a potter's field in Jerusalem several centuries later. More poppies, many tombstones, another
museum (mostly pottery), and most poignant, the
thought that this is the place where Perikles delivered
his famous funeral oration. The words he pronounced
here in 431 B.C. over the bodies of the dead Athenian
soldiers have been remembered and cherished just
as Lincoln's words at Gettysburg.

If all this sounds like rather too much walking in
the heat of the day—and it certainly is—make two
separate excursions, early or late. Or just take a seat
on a marble block on the Acropolis between the
Propylaea and the Erechtheion, look out over the
Agora, imagine the great procession to Athena crossing the Agora below you, winding up the ramp to the
Acropolis, and entering the east portico of the Parthenon—the maidens bearing the sacred robe, the city
elders, the youths on horseback, other boys carrying
water jugs, the musicians, the sacrificial animals—all
the pomp and splendor, the youth and freshness
which you have seen immortalized in the frieze from
the Parthenon in the Acropolis Museum. Then take
from your pocket a copy of Thucydides and read
Perikles' oration. One excerpt:

Our constitution does not copy the laws of neighboring states; we are rather a pattern to others than imitators
ourselves. Its administration favors the many instead of
the few; this is why we are called a democracy. If we

look to the laws, they afford equal justice to all in their private differences; if to social standing, advancement in public life falls to reputation for capacity, class considerations not being allowed to interfere with merit; nor again does poverty bar the way, if a man is able to serve the state, he is not hindered by the obscurity of his condition. The freedom which we enjoy in our government extends also to our ordinary life. There, far from exercising a jealous surveillance over each other, we do not feel called upon to be angry with our neighbor for doing what he likes, or even to indulge in those injurious looks which cannot fail to be offensive, although they inflict no positive penalty. But all this ease in our private relations does not make us lawless as citizens. Against this, fear is our chief safeguard, teaching us to obey the magistrates and the laws, particularly as regard the protection of the injured, whether they are actually on the statute book, or belong to that code which although unwritten, yet cannot be broken without acknowledged disgrace.

Further, we provide plenty of means for the mind to refresh itself from business. We celebrate games and sacrifices all year round, and the elegance of our private establishments forms a daily source of pleasure and helps to banish the spleen; while the magnitude of our city draws the produce of the world into our harbor, so that to the Athenian the fruits of other countries are as familiar a luxury as those of his own.

If we turn to our military policy, there also we differ from our antagonists. We throw open our city to the world, and never by alien acts exclude foreigners from any opportunity of learning or observing, although the eyes of an enemy may occasionally profit by our liberality; trusting less in system and policy than to the native spirit of our citizens; while in education, where our rivals from their very cradles by a painful discipline seek after manliness, at Athens we live exactly as we please, and yet are just as ready to encounter every legitimate danger.

In short, I maintain that the commonwealth of Athens is the school of Hellas, and that the individual Athenian will never meet his equal for self-reliance, versatility and gallantry in whatever situation he may find himself . . .

(Translation by R. Crawley)

These were the principles of the Athenian state at its moment of greatest glory, just as they are our ideals in this country today, however much we, like the Athenians, sometimes fall short of achieving them.

THE TEMPLE OF OLYMPIAN ZEUS

You will undoubtedly drive by the Temple of Olympian Zeus several times on your way to and from the Acropolis before you decide to stop to see it. These enormous columns, standing isolated in a field so near a busy avenue, arrest the attention and provide a magnificent spectacle at night when they are flood-lit.

It is only by walking among them, however, that you can get an idea of the size of the columns, 55.5 feet high and over 5 feet in diameter. Man is dwarfed by this, the largest temple ever built in mainland Greece. Fifteen columns remain standing out of the original

104, and one column lies tumbled on the ground, enabling you to measure yourself against its drums and to peer inside and observe how the drums were put together. They were held by iron clamps, around which lead was poured to hold the iron tight and protect it from rust. Much of the vandalism that destroyed Greek temples through the centuries was aimed at just these little bits of lead, which went to make bullets, as the marble went to make lime. That is how, or why, the mightly are fallen, though in the case of this column at the Temple of Zeus, it was a hurricane that toppled the columns, and elsewhere often an earthquake.

Peisistratos, tyrant of Athens in the sixth century B.C., first projected a colossal temple on this spot. When he died, work was abandoned, then taken up in the second century under a Syrian king, Antiochus; abandoned again, and finished under the Roman Emperor Hadrian, in the second century A.D.—a building history more like that of the Gothic cathedrals than most Greek temples, which were often built in a few years or decades.

For all that the word "colossal" has been debased by Hollywood, and may not jibe with our sense of what is fitting in a Greek temple, this great temple to Zeus has real elegance of proportion and good workmanship in its Corinthian columns. Hadrian wanted the biggest and the best, and what he got was very good indeed. Peisistratos had wanted something very big, too. It is incorrect to think of the Greeks as always measured, rational, hewing to the golden mean. Even in the perfect Classicism of the fifth century they liked the grandiose; witness Pheidias' huge statues of Athena in the Parthenon and of Zeus at Olympia, both now mercifully lost, but revered universally by the ancient world. They had their dark sides too, as the orgiastic cult of Dionysios shows. Ancient Greece was much more complex and varied than the nineteenth-century schoolmaster, from whom we have inherited many of our notions, would allow.

MONUMENT OF LYSIKRATES

The Choragic Monument of Lysikrates is most easily seen after a visit to the Temple of Olympian Zeus. Go under Hadrian's Arch, cross the boulevard and walk a block or two up Lysikrates Street (ΟΔΟΣ ΛΥΣΙΚΡΑΤΟΥΣ). There in a little square is the monument, the only one remaining of many that once lined the Street of the Tripods (ΟΔΟΣ ΤΡΠΟΔΩΝ), which in ancient times led from the Agora to the Theater of Dionysios. A *choragos* was a wealthy citizen who was chosen, and obliged as a civic duty, to pay for and direct the training of a chorus for the competition at the Dionysiac Festivals. The *choragos* of the victorious chorus was awarded a bronze tripod which he placed upon a suitable monument with a suitable inscription. Lysikrates' monument was erected in 335 B.C., according to the inscription. No, it does not say 335 B.C.! It gives the name of the archon; scholarly arithmetic does the rest.

This monument is preserved because it was incorporated into the library of a French Capuchin monastery, which looked out upon the garden, now the square. Here Byron stayed on his first trip to Greece in 1810–11, as a small stone tablet attests, but the monastery burned in the War of Independence, and the monument is now free-standing, its beauty visible from all sides.

It is a small marble rotunda, ornate and graceful, with six Corinthian columns placed between marble plaques. The frieze bears a delicate bas-relief. Dionysios is caressing his panther (a motif that also appears in mosaics at Delos) and is being served wine by young satyrs. Other satyrs are chasing pirates whom the god transforms into dolphins. The bronze tripod no longer stands on top, which is perhaps just as well.

This lovely little building is the epitome of late Classic grace. It will seem especially familiar to anyone who knows Burlington, Vermont. The cupola of the First Congregational Church there is a replica of Lysikrates' monument and very fine it looks, whether in Vermont or in Athens.

You are now close under the east side of the Acropolis in the old section of Athens known as the Plaka;

and if you are not too tired, you may follow the
picturesque and winding streets north and west to
the Roman Agora and the Tower of the Winds. If
you need a rest at this point, buses and taxis are at
hand back on the boulevard.

THE TOWER OF THE WINDS

On your walks through the Plaka you should make
a point of seeing the Tower of the Winds, near the
Roman Agora and Hadrian's Library. The latter are
too much ruined to be very interesting, but the Tower
of the Winds shows that the Romans in Athens could
and did build on the small scale as well as the large.
The tower is a marble octagon about 35 feet high.
There is a sculptured frieze around the top, each side
showing allegorically one of the eight winds and
the seasonal variations they bring. The interior originally contained a water clock, with water brought in
by aqueducts from a spring. In the Middle Ages it
was alleged to be the Tomb of Sokrates,* and in the
early eighteenth century, under the Turks, it housed
a sect of Whirling Dervishes, all of which goes to
make a sort of capsule history of post-Classical and
pre-modern Athens, except for the Byzantine, to which
we now direct you.

* At the same time the Monument of Lysikrates was thought to
be Demosthenes' study.

THE LITTLE METROPOLIS

To our minds the Byzantine appears at its best in miniature, so to speak, as seen in the three little mediaeval Byzantine churches in the heart of Athens. The loveliest of these is Agios Eleftherios, called the Little Metropolis, which sits in the shadow of the nineteenth-century Metropolitan Cathedral, and by its beauty puts its large and ugly neighbor to shame. It is made of Pentelic marble which has weathered to a soft rosy-tan. The twelfth-century builders incorporated into the fabric many of the classical stones lying about, so that in addition to the pleasure one takes in its lines and material, there is the added fascination of spotting a classical inscription here, a bas-relief there, even a Corinthian capital. On the façade, at the side of Byzantine crosses and Frankish coats of arms, there is a frieze depicting the signs of the zodiac and the principal religious feasts of antiquity. Yet it all blends together, and this little church is a delight.

Another church of similar size and period is the Kapnikarea, a block or two away on Hermes Street (ΟΔΟΣ ΕΡΜΟΥ), with its interesting double porch. And it is less than a ten-minute walk to Klafthamonos Square and the third "little gem," the Church of the Two Theodores, built of alternating courses of stone and flat brick, and decorated with a curious terra-cotta frieze showing Arab influence. Since it is the exterior of these churches which is of most interest, they can easily be seen on your way to or from some other objective.

Klafthamonos Square has an endearing tale. In the storybook days of King Otto, the Bavarian prince whom the Greeks called to the throne after they achieved independence in the 1830's, some civil servants, protesting a summary dismissal, gathered in this square, and wept. Times change.

THE OLD MARKET

Beyond Hadrian's Library, on Pandrosson Street (ΟΔΟΣ ΠΑΝΔΡΟΣΟΥ) and Hephaestos Street (ΟΔΟΣ ΗΦΑΙΣΤΟΥ) is the old craftsmen's quarter, where in little shops bordering narrow alleys men make Turkish slippers and those gay red shoes with pompoms worn by the Evzones. They come in all sizes, down to some which would fit your little girl's doll, and they make good souvenirs. Other stalls have embroideries; metalworkers display their wares; and antique coins can be found. If you pick carefully and eschew the junk, shopping here can be better and more fun than in the modern shops, which really offer very little that you would want to give house room to, let alone suitcase room.

KAISARIANI

Just ten minutes from Athens on the lower slopes of Mount Hymettos is the former monastery of Kaisariani. It is set among pines and cypresses on the site of an ancient temple to Aphrodite, some columns of which are incorporated into the tenth-century church. Ovid sang of the spring whose waters were once piped into Athens:

Est prope purpureos colles florentis Hymetti,
Fons sacer et viridi cespite mollis humus,
Silva nemus non alta facit, tegit arbutus herbam,
*Ros maris et lauri nigraque myrtus olent.**

The sacred spring still flows in the courtyard and waters the gardens, where we found maidenhair fern, which must be a rarity in Greece. The rosemary and the laurel still perfume the air, and Hymettos still catches the rosy glow of the setting sun.

Everything is on a small scale: church, refectory, and monks' quarters, and everything is completely charming. Nature seems to have blessed this spot with her smiling face. The monks who retreated here must have practiced a sunnier religion than their brothers who chose the *farouche* heights of Meteora and Mount Athos. In this green and pleasant enclave it is easy to dream of eternal peace.

---

* Near the purple slopes of flowering Hymettos there is a sacred spring with grassy banks. All around are low-growing shrubs; not a forest, but a woodland brake, where the strawberry tree, the arbutus, grows. Rosemary, myrtle, and dark-leaved laurel perfume the air. (*Art of Love*, III, 687 ff.)

LYKABETTOS

On some clear day, when you have the lay of the Athenian land fairly well in mind, you will want to spend an hour or two on Mount Lykabettos. The monastery at the top is of no particular interest, but the panorama is. There are several platforms, on different levels, facing in different directions, and refreshments are available. It is now relatively easy to get there via the underground inclined railway that takes off from the south base of the mountain and bores up through it. It is not quite so easy to find the takeoff point. Better take a taxi; by now most taxi drivers should know how to reach the entrance, but it could be a hot business on foot.

6

AEGINA
_____

ΑΙΓΙΝΑ

POROS
_____

ΠΟΡΟΣ

HYDRA
_____

ΥΔΡΑ

Famous too is Aegina, renowned for her navy . . . They never transgress right, nor yet the justice due to strangers; on the sea they are a match for dolphins in prowess, and they are wise ministrants of the Muses and of athletic contests.

PINDAR, *Fragment 1*

After two or three days in Athens, treat yourself to a day at sea among the islands of the Saronic Gulf. Here for once a cruise is a reasonable possibility: the one-day excursion to Aegina and Hydra, available from any travel agent for $10. A bus leaves early in the morning from the front entrance of the Athénée Palace Hotel and takes you to Piraeus, where you embark for Aegina, a large island whose distinctive profile, topped by the pyramidal peak of Mount Saint Elias, is a familiar and lovely sight from Athens and along the Attic coast as far as Cape Sounion.

Aegina was a prosperous trading center in the sixth century; it produced the first coinage in Europe. Because of its geographical position athwart the sea routes, it was a thorn in the side of Athens. Perikles used a different metaphor; he called it "the eyesore of

79

Piraeus." Athens' attempts to conquer Aegina were halted by the Persian Wars, when Aegina's thirty ships played a distinguished part in the victory at Salamis. But the truce was a short one. In 455 Aegina fell to Athens and had to accept harsh terms. In 431, at the start of the Peloponnesian War, Athens expelled the inhabitants of Aegina and colonized the island with Athenians. They played rough in those days, especially glorious Athens. Later the Spartans helped the Aeginetans to return to their homeland, but Aegina's role in history was over.

It is now a pleasant pastoral island, visited by tourists chiefly for its ruined temple. The beaches at Agia Marina below the temple have recently been developed, as the word is, to provide recreation for weekenders from Athens. So far the developments have not encroached on the temple, and they have increased boat service from Piraeus, with the result that it is now possible to visit Aegina comfortably without embarking on the C.H.A.T. cruise that continues to sadly overdeveloped Hydra.*

Aegina's Temple of Aphaia is one of the great temples of the Archaic period, and enjoys what must be one of the most beautiful sites in the whole world. It stands on the crest of a hill looking down over two

---

* With good management and better luck, you can go from Aegina to Poros by island steamer, take a launch (fare: ten drachmas) across the strait to Galata and a taxi to Troezen, visit the birthplace of Theseus, and catch a boat (possibly an aquafoil) back to Piraeus the same day. Since one does not always have the requisite luck, we have discussed Troezen in Chapter 11.

bays. From its steps one looks east to the blue mountains of Attica, across the blue seas of the Saronic
Gulf, then down onto the white line of the shore as it
curves around a cove, and nearer still, over the topmost boughs of a forest of long-needle pines. Here is
grandeur, not austere, but in perfect harmony with
human aspirations.

The temple is worthy of its site. Twenty-four columns have been re-erected, simple Doric columns of
local limestone, their capitals unadorned. The beauty
is all in the line and proportion. The ratio of 5 to 1
in height to diameter of the columns falls somewhere
between that of the older and sturdier Temple of
Apollo at Corinth and the Doric temples of Classical
times. In Ionic columns the ratio is higher, 6½ or 7
to 1.

This temple is unique in that the archaelogists have
been able to re-erect some of the second-story columns. Originally the interior colonnade in those temples large enough to have one, such as the Parthenon
and the Temple of Zeus at Olympia, was composed
of two tiers of columns, one above the other. Since
the roof was pitched, and therefore higher over the
interior colonnade, a single column of the height necessary to reach the roof would have been much too
large at the base, aesthetically bad, and too wasteful
of space. Vestiges of this second story can be seen
now only on Aegina and in one of the temples to Hera
at Paestum in Italy.

The temple was built between 500 and 480 B.C. Its dedication to the goddess Aphaia, a local deity related to Artemis or the Cretan Britomartis, as recounted by Pausanias, was confirmed by an inscription found in 1901 by the German archaeologist Furtwängler. His son Wilhelm, who was born on Aegina during the excavations, grew up to become the famous orchestra conductor. Furtwängler père uncovered some fragments from the pediments of an earlier temple on the same site, which can be seen in the National Archaeological Museum in Athens. But the great pediments from Aegina are now in the Munich Glyptothek. They were uncovered in 1811 by Cockerell and von Hallerstein, friends of Byron, and like him, pioneer travelers in uncharted Greece when it was still a Turkish province. The pediments were purchased by Prince Louis of Bavaria. Most books on Greek art have pictures of them, for they are among the best examples of Archaic sculpture, especially the Herakles, kneeling with drawn bow, strong but not stiff, tense and dynamic.

For the trip to the temple one disembarks at the little harbor of Agia Marina. The tour provides a bus for the short ride to the temple; taxis and donkeys are also available. A donkey ride is not comfortable; the hard wooden saddle cuts into your thighs, unless you ride sidesaddle like the natives. But if you take one for the downhill trip, and purposely lag behind, you do have a chance to be alone for a few minutes on a rocky path among the olive trees, and take a long look at the sea below.

POROS

The long island of Poros hugs the mainland of the Peloponnesos, making a narrow strait of calm waters which reflect the houses rising directly from the water's edge. No doubt the village of Poros is not so heavenly to live in as it is to look at from the decks of a passing steamer, but the Poriots must take some pleasure in the beauty that nature and man have contrived—the square white houses of Poros town, the vivid yellow and blues of the nets spread to dry on the quayside. "Art and nature thus allied . . ."

On the mainland side the little ferry landing called Galata is set in a green oasis of Lombardy poplars, whose minaret-like silhouettes give a Turkish aspect, soft and lush, to that bit of landscape. Then the eye follows the long line of the famous lemon groves up and back to the bare Argive mountains. In May the scent of the lemon blossoms delights still another sense. Henry Miller in his book on Greece, *The Colossus of Maroussi,* speaks of "the madness which is in their fragrance." The straits of Poros intoxicated Miller. "Yonder, where the mainland curls like a ship, lie the lemon groves and there in the Spring young and old go mad from the fragrance of the sap and blossom. You enter the harbor of Poros swaying and swirling, a gentle idiot tossed about amidst masts and nets in a world which only the painter knows and which he had made live again because like you, when he first saw this world, he was drunk and happy and carefree. To sail slowly through the streets of Poros is to recapture the joy of passing through the neck of the womb. It is a joy almost too deep to be remembered."

Well, almost.

Ahead lies an inlet where goats graze amid fortifications—Frankish, Turkish, Venetian? We can't say. Then one rounds the headland called Cape Skylli, named after the princess Skylla, daughter of King Nisos of Megara, who for love of Minos, the Cretan king, betrayed her father's city. King Nisos had a purple lock of hair, which, as long as it stayed on his head, protected the city. Skylla cut it and gave it as a love-token to King Minos, and the city fell. She sailed for Crete with her lover, but when he discovered her treachery to her father, he was so outraged that he had her thrown overboard near this spot which bears her name.

HYDRA

Hydra has become a place to be avoided, for reasons we will discuss; but if you take the tour to Aegina, you will be taken to Hydra willy-nilly. Once travel agents get in their heads the notion that a given place is a place to see, it takes several generations to disabuse them of it. So you might as well try to enjoy it.

It is strange, even eerie, to sail along the island of Hydra, because for some miles there is nothing on this great bare brown rock but one or two white specks way high up which seen through the glasses turn out to be monasteries. Just as on Mount Hymettos, so close to Athens and also bare of habitation, the answer is simple: no water. Hydra was absolutely uninhabited all through Classical times and the first fourteen centuries of our era. In 1460, the year the Turks conquered the Peloponnesos, a small band of Albanian shepherds which had been wandering in flight from the Turks for over a century sought a last refuge on Hydra, preferring the struggle with the natural desolation of the island to Turkish oppression.

For some years the Turks did not even suspect their presence there, and no matter how hard life was, no one's head wound up on a pile of skulls, none of their sons was conscripted as a Janizary, and there were no taxes to pay to the pasha. In the sixteenth and seventeenth centuries other settlers came from various parts of Greece. Their names were to become famous for their part in the Greek War of Independence, and are still proudly borne by Hydriots today— Kondouriotis, Tombazis, Tsamados, Oikonomou, Vokou, and Ghika (the foremost painter in Greece today is Nicoli Ghika, a native of Hydra).

The ship at last passes beneath a fort and enters a small, deep harbor. One is surprised to find a lovely town hidden there, its tall square houses climbing the hills like the steps of a giant amphitheater. Hydra has been discovered not only by tourists but by beatniks.

Rich Athenians and other foreigners have bought many of the old houses and lovingly restored them. It now rivals Mykonos as a *fais comme voudras* vacation spot. Although more colorful than Mykonos, it is not so attractive. At the risk of betraying a horrid Anglo-Saxon attitude, it is not so clean. Its beatniks are a scurvy lot, and its shopkeepers (many of them also beat) are unpleasantly aggressive. However, it is much easier to get to than Mykonos. There is even a Hydrofoil Express which makes the trip from Athens in sixty-five minutes, stopping at Poros on the way.

Just a step from the quay there is a mildly interesting monastery church, full of silver chandeliers and votive offerings. The Tombazis house (now a school of fine arts) and the Kondouriotis house above it on the hill are shown at certain hours in summer.

Until the other day, the story of Hydra was a story of daring, patriotism, and sacrifice, spiced by a dash of piracy. In 1769 an earthquake, followed by plague, laid waste the old town. The Hydriots built a new town down by the sea, and more important, kept on building ships, and more ships. During the Napoleonic wars, when the British fleet was blockading the ports of Europe, Hydriot shipmasters acquired immense fortunes by running wheat from the Crimea through the blockade in their fast little brigs. It was a dangerous game, but it paid off. It is said that Lazarus Kondouriotis kept a million gold drachma pieces hiddent in his water cistern.

With their new wealth these families built the mansions which adorn Hydra today with their austere and elegant beauty. Prosperity came to Hydra, but not peace. In 1821, when the Greeks rose against the Turks, Hydra, with the islands of Spetsai and Psara, formed a small navy that for six years fought against the overwhelmingly larger Turkish fleet, and incredibly, kept command of the sea.

A Hydriot seaman named Andreas Vokou, who had served an apprenticeship with the Barbary corsairs, became admiral of the fleet. He has come down in history under his nickname, Miaoulis, which is not a cat's miaow, but is either from the Turkish *Miaoul,* a "felucca," or from the two Greek words, *mia oulis,* meaning "one stroke," a command he may well have given to the rowers of a longboat pulling away from a Turkish man-o-war they had just set on fire. For one of his characteristic tactics was the use of fireboats—small boats filled with turpentine and gunpowder which were fastened to the enemy ship and set afire—a near-suicide operation, but one with which the Greeks had great success. The most spectacular instance was in June, 1822, soon after the massacre of Chios, a slaughter of unimaginable horror in which the Turks killed or sold into slavery almost all of the 100,000 inhabitants of that island. The French artist Eugene Delacroix made it the subject of a painting, *Le Massacre de Scio,* which with Byron's appeal from Missolonghi, did much to arouse the conscience of the West. Konstantinos Kanaris, a naval captain from the island of Psara, commanded the fireboat which blew up the Turkish flagship and almost all the Turkish captains as they were gathered aboard her to celebrate the end of the fast of Ramadan.

Admiral Miaoulis, his pitifully small navy plagued by supply problems and the fading away of volunteers (problems familiar to George Washington) could not prevent the massacre of Psara, where 20,000 were killed; but at the Battle of Yeronda his 80 Greek ships scattered and defeated the 350 heavier and better-armed Turkish and Egyptian ships.

When it was all over, Greece was free, and Hydra was bankrupt. It has been estimated that Lazarus Kondouriotis paid 5 percent of the total cost of the War of Independence out of his own pocket.

For the next century and a quarter Hydra slept again. Just a small Greek island, barren and poverty-stricken. Even its sponge-fishing industry was dying when the movie directors and the tourists came and shattered the silence. Miaoulis' cannon still guard the harbor and boom out on that day in June when the festival of the Miaoulia is celebrated. The golden casket containing the hero's heart is carried in procession from the Nautical Museum to the cathedral over streets strewn with flowers. As the day wears on, prayers and speeches give way to dancing and fireworks. This would be a day to be on Hydra.

7

ATTIC

EXTRAS

Thrice happy he among the favored few
To whom 'tis given those glorious rites to view.
Homeric Hymn to Demeter

PIRAEUS (ΠΕΙΡΑΙΕΥΣ)

Your boat trips to Aegina and Mykonos will probably show you all you want to see of Piraeus as a port, and pretty nearly all you will want to see of it as a town. It is like a plunge into the Lower East Side of New York of forty years ago. Yet there are tourist attractions there, too, not even counting those charming brothels you have seen in the movies.

Most important is the Archaeological Museum. It is a recurrent cry of the Piraeus Communist press that the museum is deliberately kept on short funds to prevent tourists from spending money in the presumably Communist-dominated port, or to deny the workers the benefits of culture, or for other dark reasons. However all this may be, we can testify that at least some of the workers are indifferent to the campaign. Being in a hurry, we took a taxi from the

Piraeus subway terminal and had to show the driver how to get there; he had heard of the theater close by, but never of the museum.

You will note that we took the subway (from Omonia Square in Athens): fast, easy, and inexpensive. If you have time and a good street map, like the one in Hachette's, you can then walk to the museum. Make allowance for the possibility that the museum may close earlier than the time announced by the Tourist Office. It did on the day we went, but a fervent plea in pidgin French that we were returning to America the next day persuaded the caretaker to open up again.

It is small, but full of wonderful things. Perhaps the most remarkable are the bronze statues of Athena and Artemis that were dug up a few years ago when a new sewer was being installed. These statues were apparently being readied for shipment to Rome (about 85 B.C.) and were saved for posterity through some kind of disaster to the warehouse where they were stored. They are still lying on their backs because, as the Communists say, the museum lacks funds to prepare them for display.

There are also four striking marble panels, two practically identical, showing scenes from the great battle between the Athenians and the Amazons, as originally depicted on the shield of the Parthenon's Athena. These, too, were probably intended to grace Roman villas.

In addition there are several beautiful grave stcle and a lovely, if much mutilated, Aphrodite, and many other odds and ends that would be the making of any museum outside of Greece. All in all a place to visit.

The Hellenistic theater is practically next door to the museum, and a somewhat commercialized program of folk dancing is put on there almost every evening. You will probably enjoy it; the only trouble is that you will have three or four hours to kill between the closing of the museum and the opening of the theater.

One solution is to stroll down the hill past the theater to the yacht basin of Pasha Limani (the ancient port of Zea), then around Point Alexandra to the harbor of Tourkolimani (ancient Munychia). It is from here that you will probably sail if you charter a yacht. And here you can dine at one of the open-air restaurants laid out in a continuous strip along the quay. Quite pleasant; but it was here and only here in all of Greece that we were conscious of being played for suckers. If this ever was the unspoiled fishing village some books describe, it is not now. John Spyrakis, the travel agent, says he knows of a really good and reasonable Tourkolimani restaurant; you should consult him before you go. In any case, after dinner take a taxi to the theater, because you will not have time to walk back.

SOUNION (ΣΟΥΝΙΟΝ)

One of the most publicized of Greek tourist attractions is Sounion, whose Temple of Poseidon has graced many an advertisement and the jacket of many a book. It was, moreover, visited by Byron, who scratched his name on it and who sang, more or less paraphrasing Sophokles:

> *Place me on Sunium's marbled steep,*
> *Where nothing, save the waves and I,*
> *May hear our mutual murmurs sweep:*
> *There, swan-like, let me sing and die!*

Sounion is set high on the promontory that is the southwest tip of Attica. For seafarers it was the last, and the first, glimpse of home.

It is easily reached from Athens—and there is the rub. For 90 drachmas (150 including dinner) you can get on a bus at the Athénée Palace at four in the afternoon, see Sounion at sunset (more or less), and be back on Constitution Square by nine thirty. You and a couple of hundred others. Camera bugs have the most fun, because they stalk each other all over the place, trying to steal a shot disfigured by no more than a dozen other photographers who also want to be alone.

If you have your own transportation, you can avoid most of this, either by visiting Sounion at some hour other than sunset (why would not dawn give about the same effect?) or by outwaiting the tour buses, which have to make that scenic drive along the Saronic Gulf and get back to Athens. If you see the sun set at Sounion, you can still make the Asteria Beach Hotel in Glyphada in plenty of time for dinner (and it will be one of the best you will have in Greece). Or you can eat at the new hotel in the cove below Sounion itself. Or—and this we diffidently recommend— you can leave Sounion to your next trip: the travel posters do not understate its glory.

LAURION (ΛΑΥΡΙΟΝ) AND BRAURON (ΒΡΑΥΡΩΝ)

If you will go to Sounion, make something of it by going or coming by way of Laurion and Brauron.

Laurion is the site of the silver mines that were a major source of wealth of Classical Athens. Mining is still done there today (zinc instead of silver) and it is as bleak as mining country anywhere. If you are bemused by the glory that was Greece, you may usefully drive through here and think on these mines. In ancient times they were worked by slaves, who were literally worked to death. Aristotle considered it natural, and no one else gave it a thought.

Beyond Laurion, up roads that can stand the improvement that some of them are now gradually getting, lies Porto Raphti, once a point of disembarkation for Delos, two millennia later an exit port for the British army, soon (if one can believe the billboards) to become the Attic Levittown. Brauron (Vravrona in modern Greek) is a few kilometers beyond, in as pretty a little valley as there is in Attica.

Brauron has a temple to Artemis, finds from which you will have seen in the National Museum; ruins of a "paleo-Christian" church; and the tomb of Iphigenia, daughter of Agamemnon and Klytemnestra. The guidebooks refer to the tomb as a cave. Perhaps it once was, but all there is now is a cleft in the rocks at the base of the hill behind the temple.*

In Classical times, Artemis seems to have been served at her temple by little girls of five to ten—and perhaps boys too—who were called "bears" (because a bear sacred to Artemis had anciently been killed in the neighborhood)—the first Cub Scouts, one might say.

DAPHNE (ΔΑΦΝΙ)

A few miles beyond the outskirts of Athens on the Eleusis road lies the former Byzantine monastery of Daphne. The fastest way is to take Achilleos Street to Leoforos Athinon to the new auto route. You will pass by the site of Plato's Academy, where once the

---

* Iphigenia was said by Aeschylus and Sophokles to have died on the altar at Aulis, but by Euripides and Apollodoros to have been spirited away by Artemis to Tauris in the Crimea, whence Orestes brought her to Brauron, where she ended her days as priestess of the temple.

philosopher and his pupils walked and talked under the trees, but now made hideous by the concrete of industry. You may want to return to Athens by the Sacred Way, Odos Iera, which you can enter right by the monastery gates.

Daphne is famous for its eleventh-century mosaics and frescoes, which have been carefully restored. The figures stand stiff on their background of gold. The iconography is similar to that of Western churches: scenes from the life of Christ and the Virgin; there is a Pentecost, or Gift of Tongues, as at Vézelay and elsewhere in France; but the placement and the emphasis are different. The Crucifixion has a relatively minor role, and the central position in the dome is given to the great Christ Pantocrator (the All-Ruler), who looks down in His terrible Majesty. This Pantocrator is regarded as one of the finest expressions of Byzantine art. We might as well say straight out that we did not like this scowling, threatening God, and much preferred some of the faded sixteenth-century frescoes, especially an early church father (Gregory?) in a side chapel to the right. His fine dark head stands out from the white of his robes and of the plaster background. With his grave but tender expression he seems to be the representation par excellence of a holy man.

Because the mosaics and frescoes at Daphne were plastered over by the Turks and have had to be uncovered, the interior of this church is atypical in that there are blank spaces on the walls. If you are an enthusiast of the Byzantine, you will want to stop at Ossias Loukas on the way to Delphi. There, every inch of the interior is covered with mosaics or dark panels of variegated marble. It is not to our taste, but considered great by everyone else.

The church and cloisters at Daphne are lovely in their soft red stone. The fleur-de-lis cotter pins on the façade recall Othon de la Roche, Duke of Athens* in the thirteenth century, who was buried there. Shakespeare was not so fanciful when he set his *Midsummer Night's Dream,* with its revels of the Duke of Athens, in the forest of Daphne.

Nearby in a shady park is a pavilion serving good, simple food. Folk dancing is performed here on summer evenings, and in September there is a Wine Festival. For a small entrance fee you can drink all the Greek wine you can hold, and join in the general merriment. As Alcaeus had it:

> *Soak your lungs with wine, for now*
> *The Dog Star's at the turn.*
> *How the summer wounds, and how*
> *All must thirst and burn.*
>   (Translation by C. M. Bowra)

ELEUSIS (ΕΛΕΥΣΙΣ)

Eleusis is notorious for its unattractive surroundings. What must once have been a beautiful outlook over

---

* Those who are surprised to find French dukes in Athens will discover more about them on p. 131 ff.

Salamis and the bay is now blighted by an unremark-able early-industrial slum, and the clear blue sky is often obscured by smoke from nearby refineries and cement plants. But no one can blame the Greeks for wanting to live on something other than tourism.

Readers of Mary Renault's *The King Must Die* will find Eleusis an exciting place. There is the spot where Theseus wrestled with the doomed king-for-a-year, and there the cave where he mated with the queen. The cave is an awesome spot in any case, for it is the mouth of the Underworld, through which Persephone (or Kore) must go to spend the winters with Hades and whence she emerges each spring to be with her mother, Demeter, in the world of light.

The Eleusian mysteries were originally a fertility rite; and arguing by analogy from the universal fate of corn kings, one can believe that something like what Mary Renault describes was once enacted here. Yet here as elsewhere all this was changed, perhaps by Theseus himself, and by historical times even the memory of the cruel drama had been lost. The nearest thing to an orgy seems to have been some rowdy shouting of naughty words as the semi-annual sacred procession proceeded from Athens and back. *Sic transit . . .*

If anything, the mysteries gained in strength from being tamed. A mark of their power is the fact that no one of the thousands upon thousands of initiates from all over the ancient world ever cared or dared to reveal them. Even the Christian fathers, in the mysteries' declining days, were able only to guess at what they were denouncing. The secret must have been incomparably moving to have been so well kept by so many for so long. Pausanias says: "My dream forbade the description of the things within the wall of the sanctuary, and the uninitiated are of course not permitted to learn that which they are prevented from seeing."

While details of the rites are lost, scholars agree that in form they were a pantomime, or a series of pantomimes, perhaps with song. Not impossibly, the forest of columns (ultimately forty-two) that held up the roof of the Telesterion, where the rites took place, made for a religious dimness that inspired awe. At the end of the ceremony the priest elevated the cult object—probably a thin sheaf of wheat—and the initiates felt renewed and better able to face life—and death.

Though bits and pieces of Mycenaean foundations can be seen here and there, and though the great days of Eleusis were the great days of Athens, from Peisistratos through Perikles, most of the noticeable ruins are Hellenistic or Roman. Here, too, Hadrian was a great builder.

Three other places in Attica you may have heard enough about to be tempted to visit:

Pentelikon. This is the mountain from which most of the marble on the Acropolis came. It is said that the ancient quarries can be reached after a climb of an hour or so from near the end of the road. Perhaps so.

Marathon. This is where the first Persian invasion was turned back in 490 B.C. A 40-foot-high mound marks the grave of the Athenian heroes. The plain, most of which did not exist at the time of the battle, has no other features. Seeing Marathon is merely an excuse for a long drive in the country; nevertheless, the scenery is beautiful, with fields of olive trees growing in red earth.

Kiphissia. This is a suburb of Athens that was sought out in the summer, presumably because its many trees gave it an appearance of coolness. Osbert Lancaster well calls it "a 'folk museum,' as it were, of the more extravagant examples of twentieth-century domestic architecture without rival in Europe . . . built by men . . . completely uninhibited by any middleclass anxiety as to what their house-master or the neighbors would think." Not recommended.

8

DELPHI

ΔΕΛΦΟΙ

> *To Apollo, the god of Delphi, there remains*
> *the ordering of the greatest and noblest and*
> *chiefest things of all . . . He is the god who*
> *sits in the centre, on the navel of the earth,*
> *and he is the interpreter of religion to all*
> *mankind.*
>
> PLATO, *The Republic*

Zeus, who had not heard of Einstein's Theory of Relativity and the difficulties it raises over simultaneity, released two eagles, one from the east, one from the west. They met over Delphi (where their descendants can still be seen soaring), which was thus proved to be the center, the very navel of the universe.

Delphi marks the coming together of cultures, as well as of eagles. This incomparably lovely and awesome spot, with its shining cleft precipice, its pulsing springs, its dark gorges, was, even before Mycenaean times, the sacred home of Gaia, the Earth Mother worshipped by the pre-Greek inhabitants of the land. Priestesses prophesied in Gaia's name and were protected by—or perhaps served—a snake or python, who was, of course, naturally close to mother earth. Around 800 B.C. Apollo killed the python and brought

Minoan priests from his birthplace, Delos, to serve the new shrine. Priestesses continued to prophesy— though now in Apollo's name—and their ancient rocky seat preserved its natural shape through Classical times and down to the present day.

Among other things, we have here, what we shall hear of again in Mycenae and elsewhere, the triumph of the male gods of the sky and the patriarchial Greek society that worshipped them over the female gods of the earth and the matriarchal, pre-Greek society. Yet the triumph is not absolute: the female principle survives in the priestesses, their title of Pythoness, and even in the Pythian Games, held quadrennially in Delphi in memory and honor of the Python.

Nor is this all. For Apollo himself marks the coming together of cultures. Already we have seen him as a Greek god and as a Minoan. Beyond this he is evidently oriental, not unlike the Hittite Apulunas and closely related to the Phoenecian Adonis.

Nor is Apollo all. In the winter he sought a more comfortable clime and turned his sanctuary over to Dionysios, the young god from Asia Minor who drove mad many of those who worshipped him—and all of those who rejected him. Every other November fourteen or sixteen Athenian Thyiads* would walk barefoot the hundred miles to Delphi, where they were joined by a similar delegation from Delphi in revels

* So his specially chosen female devotees were called in Athens and Delphi; elsewhere they were called Maenads.

on the flanks of Parnassos. The revels consisted of dancing, wild but at the same time traditional, in the course of which the Thyiads scourged themselves and tore apart and devoured sacrificial animals into which their god had entered. The Corycian Cave, where their ceremonies reached their climax, can still be visited after a stiff climb of three or four hours.

Dionysios had no temple. But everywhere he had an altar and a place of worship—the theater. Tragedy and comedy were invented for him and written and performed in his honor.

What gave Delphi its prestige in the ancient world —it boasted neither the only nor the first oracle—was its role in the diffusion, rather than the concentration of culture. It happened that the Delphic Oracle became the one consulted by colonists seeking new homes as a result of the seventh- and the sixth-century land hunger. Successful colonies were grateful for the advice they had got, or thought they had got, from the Oracle. They sent gifts to embellish Apollo's shrine, and they honored him in their new homes in song and temple. As the fame of the Oracle spread, the number coming to consult it multiplied, the knowledge and experience of the priests increased, and thereby the wisdom of the Oracle waxed.

For the most part, at least until the Persian Wars, the Delphic Oracle served the Greeks well. It is impossible now to recapture the meaning it had, either for laymen or for priests and priestesses. Geologists are certain that there was never a cleft in the rock from which gasses escaped to bemuse and inspire the prophetesses. Pharmacologists assure us that bushels of laurel leaves would have to be chewed to induce narcosis.

We should not, however, be hasty to argue from these facts that the whole thing was a conscious fraud: the prophetic trance was probably real enough, and the gasses and laurel chewing—neither of them mentioned by early sources—may have been posited to explain it. Nor should we assume that the Athenian delegation—to take one of the most famous instances—was being cynical in approaching the Oracle a second time with a more lavish votive offering in the hope (thereupon fulfilled) of obtaining a "gentler" (the term is Herodotos') answer for the forthcoming battle with the Persians. Such behavior must have seemed, to both parties, to signalize unusual piety and devotion to the word of the god, rather than, what it seems to us, bribery at once sacrilegious and childish. If it were not so, the Oracle could scarcely have survived, as it did, for a thousand years. There is poignancy in the last oracular utterance returned to Julian the Apostate in A.D. 361:

> Go tell the king:
> The fair-wrought halls
> Have fallen to the ground;
> No longer has Phoebus a shelter here.
> The laurels are cut down;
> Even the babbling water is silent now.

In 381 Theodosius dealt the last blow by banning all non-Christian cults.

There is poignancy, too, in the frustrated political possibilities of Delphi. The First Sacred War (600–590 B.C.) made of Delphi a free city protected by the Amphictyonic* League of twelve Hellenic city-states —originally centered on Thermopylae. It is tempting to see in this the possibility of a true Hellenic confederation that might have withstood first the Romans and then the Gauls and thus preserved the glory of Greece to our own day.

This hope was dashed by the Third Sacred War (356–346 B.C.), preached by the priests to punish the sacrilege of the Phocaeans, who cultivated the sacred plain of Krissa. In order to prosecute this war Philip II of Macedon was called in to help. He helped, and he stayed, and Greek politics has been the succession of oppressors from that day almost until this.

Pausanias begins his description of Delphi, as we do, with the Marmaria. The name means marble quarry and refers to the use that later times made of the ruins. Very little of what Pausanias describes survives, and much of what survives he oddly overlooks. His most striking omission is the tholos, or round Doric temple, in the Marmaria. All the guidebooks remark solemnly that its purpose is unknown (and they say the same of the Corinthian tholos at Epidauros, whose foundations we shall see). A layman may be permitted the thought

* Literally, an association of "dwellers around."

that it is its own purpose, that such a lovely building needs no external reason for existence, that whatever gods may be can thank men for worshipping them with such works.

The other striking remain in the Marmaria is remarkable for a contrary reason; as architecture it is only moderately interesting, but its purpose is powerfully suggestive. This is the Massalian Treasury, that is, the treasury of Marseilles—a city founded by Ionians from Phocaea in Asia Minor in about 600 B.C. and rich enough by 535 to lay up wealth here under the double protection of Athena Pronaia (Athena of the Entrance) and of the great Apollo. The threads of Mediterranean culture were early tangled.

Passing through the Gymnasium, we come next to the Castalian Spring, which rises from the base of Hyampeia, the easternmost of the Phaidriades (the Shining Rocks). At this spring pilgrims purified themselves before entering the sanctuary of Apollo. From the cliff rising sheer eight or nine hundred feet overhead Delphinians were wont to cast blasphemers; the name of one has come down to us: Aesop, the fabulist, who appears to have questioned the infallibility of the priests.

The purified pilgrim went next to the agora (the interesting remains are Roman) where he might—like the pilgrim to Tinos or Lourdes today—buy a medal or an offering for the god. And then, on the Sacred Way (Roman paving again), into the sanctuary itself, a crowded five-acre tract extending up the hillside. In Pliny's day (first century A.D.) there were over 3,000 statues here, and he averred that 500 others had been stolen by Nero and that hundreds more had disappeared during the various religious wars and particularly during Sulla's occupation in 86 B.C. Thus at its height Delphi must have had upwards of 4,000 statues, some marble, some bronze, some gold. Making allowance for the space occupied by the various treasuries, the Temple of Apollo, the theater, and the Sacred Way, we are left with the appalling average of one statue for every 4 or 5 square yards. Since most of them were crowded along the 220 yards of the Sacred Way the density must have been even greater. One of several homilies inscribed in the temple was "Nothing in excess." Another might appropriately have been "Do as I say, not as I do."

This conspicuous display was brought about by a perversion of the temple's other renowned prescript: "Know thyself." With most Greeks the urge was not to look inward but to holler "Look at me!" Statues were erected by individuals to boast of victories in the games (which included singing). They were erected by families to advertise descent from some god or hero. They were erected by city-states to display the spoils of war—spoils taken sometimes from barbarians but more frequently from fellow Greeks. Thus at the very entrance of the sanctuary there was on the left the ex-voto of the Athenians in memory of

Marathon (in which Spartan troops did not partici-
pate). Facing this across the Sacred Way was the
ex-voto of the Spartans in honor of Lysandros' naval
victory over Athens at Aigos Potamoi in 405. Next to
this the Arcadians commemorated their victory over
Sparta at Leuctra in 371. Then facing each other
across the Sacred Way are two monuments of the
Argives celebrating their victories over Sparta, and
one of them flaunted spoils they had taken.

Nothing except foundations remains of all these
proud boasts. But the Athenian Treasury has been
reconstructed with the original stones (in the same
way as the Nike Temple in Athens); the original
rocks of the priestesses of Gaia still stand; and the
Athenians have another memorial in the portico they
built against the polygonal retaining wall of Apollo's
temple in order to display the cables that held Xerxes'
bridge of ships across the Hellespont at Abydos.

Before the eastern entrance of the temple stood the
great altar. Here the pilgrim made sacrifice before
approaching the Oracle. The sacrifice itself could not
be made unless the priest pronounced the omens favorable. Evidently the consultation consisted in pouring a libation over the sacrificial animal—generally
a goat—which by shuddering consented to its death
and thus bore witness to the god's presence. Plutarch,
who toward the end of the first century A.D. was a
priest of Apollo at Delphi, tells of one instance when
cynical priests kept pouring cold water on an obdurate

CORINTH   *The Temple of Apollo, with Acrocorinth in the distance*

PYLOS   *The bathtub in Nestor's Palace*

DELOS   *Mount Kythnos with the Temple of Isis (above)*

NAXOS   *Dionysios from his feet (left)*

MYKONOS   *Toward the eastern side of the harbor (facing, top)*

HYDRA   *The harbor (facing, bottom)*

OLYMPIA   *The Temple of Hera, with
a corner of the Temple of Zeus in
the left background and the
Gymnasium at the right (top, left);
Zeus Kidnapping Ganymede, Olympia
Museum (top, right)*

MYCENAE   *The Treasury of Atreus
(bottom, left); Lucile Brockway and
Aristoteles in the Lion Gate
(bottom, right)*

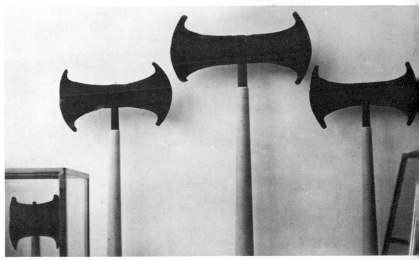

KNOSSOS   *Central staircase of the Palace of Minos (top, left); Storage jars (top, right); Bronze double-axes, Herakleion Museum (bottom, right)*   PHAESTOS   *The grand courtyard (bottom, left)*

XV

RHODES   *Entrance of the Hospital of the Knights (top)*

LINDOS   *The Temple of Athena (left)*

goat, whose final shuddering was thus natural rather than supernatural. One is perhaps entitled to suppose that the opposite sometimes happened, and that priests were able to find the omens unfavorable when they wanted to.

Very little remains of the temple, which was at least the fourth on the site and dates from the fourth century. And what remains is not altogether understood. Some guides and guidebooks mention a space they take to be the subterranean chamber of the Oracle, which is apparently connected by a passageway with the rocks of Gaia outside. Recent scholarship, however, is inclined to be skeptical.

Above the temple is the theater, a little gem (seating capacity 5,000) dating from the second century. Like the other surviving Greek theaters, it is an acoustical wonder and indeed has the acoustical center marked by a small cross in the orchestra floor. And still farther up (and outside the sanctuary) is the stadium: a new road winds through the town to the stadium's level. Unless you feel obligated to climb the steep steps because they are there, you will be well advised to drive up the road. However you get there, you should remember that our old friend Herodes Atticus was responsible for the seating arrangements.

But first you will want to return to and linger in the museum, which may or may not be the eyesore everyone says it is, but which certainly has a collection of wonders. The exhibits are well displayed but not well labeled; you will need a guide or one of the better guidebooks to make the most of them.

There are characteristically Greek stories connected with some of the exhibits. That of Kleobis and Biton (whose archaic statues have an Egyptian grandeur) is best given by Herodotos (I:31–34), who has Solon, while visiting Croesus during his self-imposed exile, cite them as among the happiest of men. "Their fortune," says Solon, "was enough for their wants, and they were besides endowed with so much bodily strength that they had both gained prizes at the Games. Alas this tale is told of them: There was a great festival in honor of Hera at Argos, to which their mother (a priestess) must needs be taken in a car. Now the oxen did not come home from the field in time; so the youths, fearful of being too late, put the yoke on their own necks and themselves drew the car five miles to the temple. . . . The mother, overjoyed at the deed and at the praises it had won, besought the goddess to bestow on Kleobis and Biton the highest blessing to which mortals can attain. Her prayer ended, they offered sacrifice, and partook of the holy banquet, after which the two youths fell asleep in the temple. They never woke more, but so passed from the earth. The Argives, looking on them as among the best of men, caused statues of them to be made, which they gave to the shrine at Delphi."

Solon's moral did not impress Croesus, "since he

thought a man must be an arrant fool who made no
account of present good, but bade men always wait
and mark the end." But, says Herodotos, "after Solon
had gone away a dreadful vengeance, sent of God,
came upon Croesus, to punish him, it is likely, for
considering himself the happiest of men." And he
ended his days as the slave of Cyrus the Great.

Did the Greeks really think death better than life?
Or did they merely feel it imprudent to tempt the
fates? It should perhaps be added that Robert Graves
sees in Kleobis and Biton a memory of human sacrifices offered when a new temple was dedicated to the
moon goddess.

A more puzzling story lies behind the scene represented on the pediment from the Siphnian Treasury,
where we see Herakles trying to make off with the
Delphic tripod in spite of opposition from Athena
and Apollo. Herakles, as he generally did, acted on
the spur of the moment, because the prophetess refused to listen to him, on the ground that he was
guilty of murdering Iphitos. The *bad* thing about that
was that he was Iphitos' host at the time. This yarn
is thought to refer to a Dorian capture of the shrine,
but it is unlikely that the Siphnians saw beyond its
typical connection of the hero with Delphi.

The Greeks, by the way, were tripod-happy: they
awarded them to winners of choral contests; they
dedicated them to gods; they stored them, by the
hundreds, in their treasuries. The prophetess evi-

dently sat on hers, and some were used to burn incense in, and some were used to hold amphorae and other jars. The rest were, in effect, for cook-outs.

We shall see a fine display of tripods in the museum at Olympia, but the base of the most famous is now in Istanbul, in the park where the Hippodrome stood, in front of the Blue Mosque. Pausanias says: "The Greeks in common dedicated from the spoils taken at the Battle of Plataea a gold tripod set on a bronze serpent. The bronze part of the offering is still preserved, but the Phocaian leaders who despoiled the shrine in 353 B.C. did not leave the gold." After Pausanias' time even the bronze base was taken away by Constantine to embellish his new capital.

9

OLYMPIA

K - ΟΛΥΜΠΙΑ

Where Alph, the sacred river, ran . . .
COLERIDGE, *Kubla Khan*

The glory of Olympia is its museum. The ruins are pleasant to wander through, especially because of the pine trees the German archaeologists planted when they finished their excavation a half century ago. But the untrained eye is not surprised by anything it sees outdoors there, with the possible exception of the Stadium. What is so unusual about the Stadium—probably the most famous in the world —is that it has embankments for the spectators but no seats. Herodes Atticus, who did take care of a fountain in the sanctuary, seems to have missed a good bet.

You should start your visit with the museum, and you should plan to spend most of your time there. It is not large, nor is it overpoweringly full. But it has these great things:

The pediments (and some of the metopes) from the Temple of Zeus;
The Winged Victory of Paionios;
The terra-cotta Zeus Kidnapping Ganymede;
The Hermes of Praxiteles.

These must be seen. None, and certainly not the first, is adequately represented by photographs. Art histories and guidebooks uniformly praise the majesty of the central Apollo in the west pediment. They are right, and photographs do not begin to show it. You will have to see for yourself.

This pediment shows centaurs trying to rape the women of Lapith (somewhere in Thessaly), Lapith men resisting them with the help of Theseus, and Apollo quelling the uproar. This stimulating episode occurred at the wedding of Peirithoös, the Lapith king, to Deidameia. The gods, with the exception of the trouble-makers Ares and Eros, also attended the wedding; but this time it was the centaurs who did not behave themselves. They were unused to wine, and one thing led to another.

All this may very well be true, but it does not go far to explain the choice of this story for the pediment of the Temple of Zeus. Pausanias also felt it needed accounting for, but the best he could do was: "Alcamenes, I think, carved this scene because he had learned from Homer's poem [*Iliad*, XIV, 318] that Peirithoös was a son of Zeus, and he knew that

Theseus was a great grandson of Pelops [shown on the east pediment]." Pausanias wrongly identified the sculptor and did not cast much light otherwise.

For some reason that we cannot discover, the story is scarcely referred to in extant literature but appears frequently on vases and on at least these buildings: the Parthenon and Hephaesteion in Athens, the Athenian Treasury in Delphi, the Temple of Apollo at Bassae, and here in Olympia. The Athenians were perhaps interested because of Theseus' role, and some think they consciously built Theseus up as a counter-weight to the fame of Argive (or Theban) Herakles. Such a theory does not take Bassae (even though an Athenian architect did build it) or Olympia into account, nor does it explain the emphasis given this particular exploit of Theseus.

Who were the centaurs anyway? Graves says they were a Neolithic mountain tribe in northern Greece. The Eleventh Edition of the *Britannica* thinks they may have been Scythians, the fierce nomadic peoples from north of the Black Sea, whose skill in fighting on horseback and whose barbaric customs are so vividly described by Herodotos (Book IV). It seems likely that the story interested sculptors not only for its movement but also as an exemplification of the struggle between Hellas and the barbarians. Beyond this, it is not impossible that a kernel of history lies somewhere in the legend, as may also be the case with the companion tale of Theseus' defeat of the Amazons at the gates of Athens. John Forsdyke (*Greece Before Homer*) identifies the Amazons with the same Scythian hordes (Scythian women dressed and rode and sometimes fought like men; Scythian men, because of long hours on horseback, were reportedly frequently impotent).

The east pediment is a static composition in startling contrast to the one we have been discussing. But its story is in its way just as wild, and it has the triple importance of accounting for the name Peloponnesos, of inspiring the Olympic Games, and of providing the original curse that doomed the House of Atreus.

King Oenomaos of Pisa (whose territory subsequently included Olympia) had a beautiful daughter, Hippodameia, whose hand he would give only to a prince who could beat him in a chariot race. As is customary with such arrangements, suitors who failed forfeited their lives, and thirteen had been dispatched when Pelops, an Asia Minor prince, son of Tantalos, resolved to win the princess.

Tantalos deserved the eternal torment that has made his name famous, because inviting the gods to dine with him, he served them his son Pelops artfully butchered and tastefully boiled. He is said to have wanted to demonstrate that the gods could be fooled. Fortunately for Pelops, he was proved wrong, but only after Demeter had eaten his left shoulder. The rest of him was put together and restored to life, and an ivory left shoulder repaired the damage.

In the course of this adventure, Pelops secured the affection of Poseidon, who eventually provided him with winged horses for the defeat of Oenomaos. But Oenomaos' horses were magic, too, being the gift of Ares; so Pelops bribed Myrtillos, Oenomaos' charioteer, to substitute wax plugs for the king's linch pins, and so the king's chariot collapsed and the king died in the wreckage. Myrtillos tried to collect his bribe—half of the kingdom and the enjoyment of Hippodameia on her wedding night—but Pelops kicked him into the sea. As he fell, he cursed Pelops and all his issue, which proved to include Atreus and Thyestes, whose accursed lot we shall hear about in Mycenae. Pelops revived the Olympic Games in his late father-in-law's memory (Herakles originally ran them, but why they were suspended is a question we do not propose to try to answer). Pelops, of course, gave his name to the land; *Peloponnese* means "Isle of Pelops," and it is certainly a *presqu'île*.

These are the people rigidly represented in the east pediment with Zeus standing in the center as a sort of master of ceremonies. He does not figure particularly in the story, but it is his temple.

Most of the metopes from the temple are in Paris (one hears a great deal about the dastardly Elgin but oddly little about Frenchmen and Germans who also knew a good thing when they saw it). The Olympia Museum, however, has some originals and plaster casts of the rest. Their subject is the Labors of Herakles and they are vigorous and lovely, with, it seems, an occasional touch of humor as befits a treatment of their erratic and irresponsible hero. While he holds up the heavens to allow Atlas to get the golden apples for him, Athena (or one of the Hesperides?) stands behind him with her left hand raised. Raised enough to catch the burden if he fumbles, but not enough to bear any of the weight in the meantime: she is willing to help him, but she does not have to trust him.

The Nike of Paionios, one of the loveliest of ancient works, was an offering of the Messenians and Naupaktians in celebration of their 420 B.C. victory over the Spartans. Its base still stands in front of the Temple of Zeus.

Zeus Kidnapping Ganymede (a Trojan prince who became his cupbearer and bedfellow), one of the most charming of ancient works, originally stood on the roof of one of the Altis treasuries.

The Hermes of Praxiteles dates from the fourth century. It is one of the most famous of ancient works, and we shall say nothing against it.

Also in the museum will be found a large collection of tripods, another of bronze shields, and a deal of Roman remains, many of them representing the family of Herodes Atticus. Before leaving the museum, you should study the plaster reconstruction of Olympia; it will make your wanderings among the ruins pleasanter and easier.

The sanctuary is called the Altis; there is no agreement on the origin of the name. We will mention in particular only two of the many things to be found there.

First and in many ways the most curious is Pheidias' workshop, where the great sculptor and friend of Perikles is thought to have fashioned his chryselephantine statue of Zeus.

The *chrys* means "golden": Zeus' robes were made of gold. The *elephantine* refers to the statue's being made partly of ivory (which was used for the flesh), not to its size, though it was a monstrous thing some 35 feet high and was counted as one of the Seven Wonders of the World. It was carted off to Constantinople by Theodosius II and destroyed in a fire in A.D. 475.

The workshop was oriented precisely as the temple, so that Pheidias would be able to tell at every stage how it would look when finally set up. Given its dimensions, this seems an excess of delicacy.

Also particularly interesting is the Heraeion, or Temple of Hera, which is one of the few ancient buildings to show traces of having been built over a span of years. It dates from the seventh century and apparently first had wooden pillars. As these rotted, they were replaced with stone, but no attempt was made to maintain a uniform style. Unlike the mediaeval cathedrals, Greek temples were usually built in a very short time. The Parthenon, including the sculpture, took fifteen years, and the entire Classical

Acropolis with Propylaea, Nike Temple, and Erechtheion, took only forty-one years. The third Temple
of Apollo at Delphi was built in eight years, and the
fourth in thirty. The Temple of Zeus here in Olympia
took only thirty-one years, including the cult statue
in all its glory.

Of course the ancient houses of worship did not
begin to compare with the mediaeval in size. This
Temple of Zeus was about 210 feet long and 91 feet
wide. The Parthenon is about 228 feet by 101. In
contrast, Chartres is 390 feet long and 193 feet wide
at the transept. Even more striking, of course, is the
difference in heights: Zeus at Olympia, 48 feet to the
top of the entablature; Parthenon, 45 feet; Chartres,
to the nave vaulting, 110 feet; to the top of the north
tower, 346 feet.

10

CLASSICAL

EXTRAS

> *Suppose the city of Sparta to become deso-*
> *late and nothing left but the temples and*
> *foundations, then posterity would be most*
> *unwilling to believe the Lacedaemonians*
> *as powerful as their reputation proclaims.*
> THUCYDIDES, *The Peloponnesian War, I, 10*

The Classical Tour can be extended, if you have the time and the inclination, to include Bassae, Karytena, Megalopolis, Ithome, Pylos, Mistra, Sparta, and Tegea, or a combination of them. They fit in more or less conveniently between Olympia and Nauplia. In the present state of the roads it takes a good four days to cover all of them; five days would be better.

Bassae (ΒΑΣΣΑΙ) is in the land of Arcady, where shepherds still pipe. Blessed with rugged mountain scenery, it is now, and probably always has been, backward and primitive rather than languorous and romantic. Your preparations should include a full gas tank and a picnic lunch.

Starting from Olympia, you must return to Pyrgos, where you turn south on the new highway that quickly proves to be unfinished. But soon you turn east for Andritsena (ΑΝΔΡΙΤΣΑΙΝΑ), and the fun begins. The road actually is no worse than that to a backwoods camp in Maine, but there are 54 kilometers of it. Ten miles an hour is a good cruising speed.

The worst parts are the two or three hilltop villages, none of which seems to have an active Department of Streets and Roads. On the other hand, none has need of a Traffic Bureau; debouching from one of them just after noon, we startled the hell out of an old gentleman who was taking his siesta stretched across the road, his head comfortably on a stone on one side, and his feet conveniently in the ditch on the other.

There are no more than two forks on the entire route. They are unmarked, but the correct turnings are fairly obvious. If in doubt you need merely ask "Andritsena?" of the first passerby you meet (accent on the second syllable).

When you have about given up hope, you reach Andritsena. From there the road to Bassae (14 kilometers) is blacktopped, but perhaps more harrowing than what went before. It is barely wide enough for two cars to pass; it has the typical Greek sharp sides without shoulders; it is a constant succession of hairpin turns, most of them blind. We leaned on our horn the whole way up and back but met only two cars, both of which surprised us. Incidentally, the official National Tourist Organization Map of Greece shows

Bassae to the north of Andritsena; it is to the south.

The temple, dedicated to Apollo, is in a wild and wonderful spot, 3,700 feet up in the middle of nowhere. It was forgotten by all except local shepherds until a French architect named Bocher stumbled across it in 1765. When he returned the next year, he was murdered by bandits. It was built by the great Ictinus, architect of the Parthenon; it was the first temple in which the Corinthian order was used (one, or Dinsmoor says three, interior columns); it alone of all Greek temples is oriented north and south rather than east and west (the books say the site dictated the orientation, but fifth-century architects solved worse problems daily); it is, with the Hephestaeion in Athens and the Temple of Aphaia on Aegina, one of the best preserved. Pausanias thought that "of the temples in the Peloponnesus, this might be placed first after the one at Tegea for the beauty of its stone and for its symmetry." Yet you must count yourself an enthusiast to want to make the trip.

If you do make it, you will spend the night in Andritsena, where there is a brand-new Xenia Hotel, which has this annoying lack: there are no reading lamps on the beds.

The next town east of Andritsena is Karytena (KAPYTAINA), which has a Frankish castle dating from the thirteenth century (A.D. this time) that is well worth a slight detour and a half hour's scramble to visit. The view over the valley of the Alpheus is magnificent, and in the spring the steep hillside is covered with wild flowers. We counted over fifty varieties. If a boy materializes and offers to guide you, retain his services regardless of the language barrier, for the path up to the castle is overgrown and vagrant.

This was the favorite seat of Geoffrey de Bruyères, a surprising transplant from mediaeval France who was the very flower of chivalry and a romantic, madcap knight; his adventures are too extensive and various to bear retailing here, except for one beguiling story. On the eve of the Battle of Pelagonia in 1259, the Despot of Epirus and the Prince of Achaea basely decided to abandon their Greek followers and flee. Geoffrey alone protested, but he was overruled, and with the other barons had to take an oath of secrecy. Once in his own tent, however, he addressed his tent pole, crying out:

"O tent pole, hold strong the tent that covers me and tell her for me that she should never disbelieve that I love her well, and that I do not require her to be in peril. We have taken counsel, the prince and the despot and the foremost of the army, to flee this evening and leave to their peril the common troops. For this reason, I say to you, my beloved tent, do not by any chance think that the matter stands otherwise; consider how you may escape your peril."

Chronicle of the Morea
(Translation by Harold E. Lurier)

Compare this with an extract from the Gilgamesh Epic of the third millennium B.C. in Mesopotamia. Ea, the good god who is friendly to mankind, wants to warn the man Utnapishtim so that he may escape the Flood which the gods are secretly preparing. He addresses not Utnapishtim, but his house:

> *"Reed hut, reed hut!*
>   *Wall, wall!*
> *Reed hut, hear!*
>   *Wall, perceive!*
> *O man of Shuruppak, son of Ubara-tutu,*
> *Tear down the house,*
>   *Build the ship."*
>   (Translation by Cyrus H. Gordon)

One is tempted to think that Geoffrey or the chronicler who told his story had seen a copy of the Gilgamesh Epic. The modern world did not even suspect its existence until the latter half of the nineteenth century, when twelve tablets were found in the library of Assurbani-pal at Nineveh.

As Geoffrey had intended, his followers overheard his words and the Franks were forced to give battle. They were defeated. Geoffrey and his lord, Guillaume de Villehardouin, were taken prisoner. In captivity Geoffrey became a favorite of the Byzantine Emperor and was ultimately released to help arrange Villehardouin's ransom—four castles, including his particular favorite, the stronghold of La Crémonie, which under the Byzantines became the great city of Mistra and was called a second Constantinople.

The consequences of Geoffrey's chivalry were grave, almost fatal, for the Franks, but no one seems to have held it against him. Indeed, he always had a way with him. Twice he offended his liege lord and violated his feudal oath—once by eloping with a vassal's wife. Both times he appeared before his peers with a halter around his neck and was forgiven. The *Chronicle of the Morea* relates that at his death in 1275 "all wept for him, great and small alike. The very birds sang songs of lamentation."

Seventeen kilometers southeast of Karytena is Megalopolis (ΜΕΓΑΛΟΠΟΛΙΣ) "the great city," built by the Arcadian League (of which it became the capital) in four years (371–67) with a view to containing Sparta. By the second century A.D., Pausanias found that it had "lost all its beauty and its old prosperity, being today for the most part in ruins." He adds: "I am not in the least surprised, as I know that heaven is always willing something new, and likewise that all things, strong or weak, increasing or decreasing, are being changed by Fortune, who drives them with imperious necessity according to her whim." If you have time, and if the side road is passable, you may want to look at the Megalapolitan theater, the largest in Greece, once capable of holding 20,000 people. You may want to take a look, and reflect on the insecurity of men's purposes.

At Megalopolis you reach a decent road again, whether you turn north for Tripolis, Argos, and Nauplia, or south for Messenia and Pylos. It is also possible to go via Tripolis to Mistra and Sparta. The first option can be run in an afternoon; the second, which we will describe briefly, requires three days or possibly four to bring you to the same place; and the third requires two days.

Ithome (IΘΩMH) was the capital of Messenia, always an enemy of Sparta, and during much of ancient times under Spartan domination. The city whose ruined walls are now visible was built by Epaminondas of Thebes in 371 as part of the system that also included Megalopolis. It remains one of the best preserved of ancient fortifications. On clear days it is visible from Bassae, only 20 miles to the north as the crow flies. But it is reached by a miserable road about 10 kilometers long that leaves the main highway about 39 kilometers south of Megalopolis. It is not recommended for your first trip.

Pylos (ΠΥΛΟΣ) has won deserved fame because the American archaeologist Carl W. Blegen discovered near there the ruins of the Palace of Nestor, Agamemnon's wise counselor in the *Iliad*. More romantic is the fact that the ruins contain the bath in which Nestor's daughter, Polykasta, bathed Odysseus' son, Telemachos, as described in Book III of the *Odyssey*. "And when she had bathed him and rubbed him with olive oil, she gave him a tunic to wear; then he stepped out of the tub, as handsome as a young god." More significant is the fact that the ruins contained some hundreds of tablets incised with the Linear B script Sir Arthur Evans had earlier found at Knossos. The palace has been neatly excavated and can be understood with the help of an excellent pamphlet available at the entrance. But its site is relatively undramatic, and it has nowhere near the interest of its contemporary, Mycenae, except for the hearth in the throne room, which, with its painting around the edge, seems almost to bring the old times back.

There is a small museum at Chora, 3 or 4 kilometers to the north, but you can never be sure when it will be open.

Modern Pylos is on the beautiful Bay of Navarino, where in 1827 a Turkish fleet was destroyed in an accidental battle with British, French, and Russian squadrons. Thereafter Greek independence was inevitable, though it was not finally attained until 1832. The bay is closed by the 3-mile-long island of Sphacteria, where an Athenian contingent forced the surrender of a Spartan garrison in 425, after a siege lasting 72 days. This was one of the few instances of Spartan surrender, and the Peloponnesian War might have ended right there, on terms favorable to Athens and, no doubt, to those of us who have lived since. But the Athenians were not generous victors, and so became humiliated losers.

There is a Xenia Hotel (also called the Hotel Nestor) in Pylos, small but pleasant. It would be a fine place for a visit of several days (there are other places of interest in the neighborhood); but it is a long, difficult drive from Andritsena, and a long, difficult drive to Sparta. A road is being built along the coast to Pyrgos; but even if this is well and quickly built, Pylos will be a place to stay several days or not at all, or to visit by yacht.

Mount Taygetos lies between Pylos and Sparta (ΣΠΑΡΤΗ). What the Greeks call a mountain, we should call a mountain range. Taygetos stretches north and south a distance of 30 miles. Its highest peak—mountain to us—is some 7,800 feet high, and it has several that are over a mile. Snow is common on them even in May.

Road maps show a firm red line over the mountain, through the Langada Pass. Do not be misled. It may by now be paved from a new tourist hotel at the pass down to Sparta; but even so the western end is still gravel, and the paved part is certainly as exciting as, say, the road from Andritsena to Bassae. We started over at ten thirty one morning and picked up Finn, our Danish hitchhiker, as we began the climb. He had been waiting for a ride since seven thirty, and we were the third vehicle—trucks included—to come along in either direction.

Do not be dismayed. The driving is not really bad;

it just takes time. At least four hours should be allowed for the trip from Pylos to Sparta. One wonders how Telemachos and Nestor's son Peisistratos made it in two days in a chariot. This was in 1175 B.C. or thereabouts. Perhaps roads were better then.

Just south of Sparta, on a foothill of Taygetos, near the one where the Spartans were wont to hurl their deformed or weakling children, is Mistra (ΜΥΣΤΡΑΣ), a Frankish-Byzantine-Venetian-Turkish city that once had a population of 42,000 but is now deserted except for a few religious, whose presence is due perhaps as much to the tourist trade as to anything. The thought of Mistra—once the scene of so much splendor, romance, and chivalry, and so much squalor, bumble, and cruelty—is possibly more fascinating than the actuality. Where one may complain of a prehistoric site like Pylos that the ruins are too scanty, here they are bewilderingly extensive. No really adequate view of them—even of the three or four fourteenth-century churches whose frescoes are in a good state of preservation—can be had in the few hours the average tourist is willing to devote to the place. But if you take this route, stop long enough to see one church, the Peribleptos, which is hard by the lunch pavilion.

It should be added that a thorough visit to Mistra requires more climbing and scrambling than any other attraction in Greece.

Thucydides was right enough in his speculation that the ruins of Sparta would not amount to much. The museum in Sparta nevertheless preserves several things worth seeing if you are in the neighborhood. Foremost is the bust of a warrior who has been identified by some unsung public relations expert as King Leonidas, hero of Thermopylae. Even if not Leonidas, he is a fine figure. Then there is a considerable series of grotesque ceremonial masks in terra cotta. Arguing from the use made of grotesque masks in Nigeria today, one may suppose that they were worn by dancers to scare off evil spirits. A few similar masks, by the way, can be seen in the museum in Nauplia.

Some 55 kilometers north of Sparta, a road to the right leads to Tegea, which Pausanias, it will be remembered, ranked ahead of Bassae. Only foundations remain, though again there is an interesting little museum.

At Tripolis, the Classical Extras route rejoins the direct route from Olympia to Nauplia. Several travel books recommend Tripolis as a center from which to visit most of the places we have been describing. Perhaps this was a sensible idea when you had to travel by railroad and there were no hotels at the end of the line. Now it is worth devoting considerable thought to be sure not to be stuck in Tripolis, which is a dreary modern village, boasting, in its Arcadia, of the second worst hotel we have ever seen anywhere.

Beyond Tripolis, on the western outskirts of the village of Myli (ΜΥΛΟΙ), on the shores of the Bay of Nauplia, is Lerna, a Neolithic (New Stone Age, i.e., about 3000 B.C.) settlement, very likely the oldest building you will see in Greece. Like Pylos, it was excavated by American archaeologists. It also requires much learning—and more imagination—to be fully appreciated. It was here, by the way, that Herakles killed the nine-headed Hydra. Graves says the myth preserves the memory of the draining of the neighboring swamp.

There are a theater and other things to see in Argos, but we have seen theaters before and shall see others soon. Let us hurry on to Nauplia, where we can relax a bit and from where we can drive out to see Mycenae.

11

MYCENAE

KZMYKHNAI

And yet the very house, if it had voice,
would speak out clear—just as I too speak out
to those who know. To those who do not—why,
I lose my memory.

AESCHYLUS, *Agamemnon*
(Translation by Edith Hamilton)

More than any other site in Greece, Mycenae must be prepared for. It is one of the richest and most exciting places in Greece—indeed, in all Europe— but only, as Aeschylus' Watchman says, to those who know. The required preparation is of two kinds; reading at home, and looking in the National Archaeological Museum in Athens.

Mycenae first seizes the imagination as the seat of the thrice-cursed House of Atreus—descendants of Pelops and Tantalos, themselves accursed, as we have already learned at Olympia. Pelops' sons Atreus and Thyestes were invited, so the legend has it, to rule in Mycenae. As might have been expected, especially in the Bronze Age when men were touchy, they quarreled. To seal an apparent reconciliation, Atreus invited his brother to a banquet. The entrée was

Thyestes' sons (Tantalos, it will be remembered, had served Pelops up to the gods).

Atreus was succeeded on the throne by his son Agamemnon, who was, says Homer, "Lord of many islands and over all Argos," while his brother Menelaos ruled Sparta and, sometimes, Helen. When unfavorable winds delayed Agamemnon's fleet's departure for Troy, he sacrificed his daughter Iphigenia to Artemis,* who had previously been overlooked (similar oversights initiated many another Greek horror tale, but the Greeks never could seem to be careful in such matters).

Agamemnon's wife, Klytemnestra, thereupon took as her lover Thyestes' son Aigisthos (whose mother was his own half sister: if this seems like a riddle, remember that it was propounded by the Delphic Oracle, who advised the incest). Ten years subsequently, when Troy had fallen, Aigisthos was Klytemnestra's accomplice in the murder of Agamemnon. Murdered with him was Priam's daughter Kassandra, part of his spoils of victory (Klytemnestra herself had been among the spoils of an earlier victory). Nine years after that, Elektra, daughter of Klytemnestra and Agamemnon, persuaded her brother Orestes to murder their mother and her paramour. Naturally the Furies pursued him because of this unnatural act, but at length his case was considered by the Athenian Council on the Areopagos and he was

* See p. 96.

acquitted, the margin being provided by Athena, who had also acted as defense counsel.

It was in the palace on the citadel of Mycenae that these murders took place, if they took place at all.*

If they did not take place, something very like them did, for Mycenae bears the scars of many civil wars.

The site has been occupied for five thousand years. The original settlers were non-Greeks—that is, they did not speak the Greek language—and are generally referred to as Pelasgians. They worshipped a fertility goddess or goddesses, practiced mysterious rites, and possibly were organized in a matriarchy.

About 2000 B.C. the first Greeks appeared in Mycenae, bringing bronze tools and weapons, the worship of Zeus, and a monarchy that was absolute, at least in time of war. The Bronze Age lasted perhaps a thousand years and saw the development of a rude but brilliant civilization centered in fortified cities, devoted at least as much to plunder as to trade, and drawing inspiration from its contacts with the older civilizations of Crete, Egypt, and the Hittites. Then as now, Mycenae was the most considerable of these cities and has given its name to the entire civilization. Agamemnon came almost at the end. The fall of Troy is traditionally dated at 1184 B.C. However that may be, within a century Mycenae, neighboring Tiryns, and all the other Bronze Age cities,

* Though Aeschylus places them at Argos.

with the possible exception of Athens, were over-whelmed and destroyed by fire.

Although there are some (notably Immanuel Velikovsky) who see this disaster the result of natural catastrophe, the accepted view has been that it was accomplished by waves of Dorians pushing down from the north and around the Peloponnesos. Like their predecessors, the Dorians were Greeks. Their metal, however, was iron, against which bronze is no match. Under them Mycenae was never more than a country village and steadily declined. In place of the hundred ships, each with fifty men, it sent to Troy, it could provide only eighty men at Thermopylae and shortly thereafter was deserted. Pausanias says the Argives destroyed Mycenae in a fit of jealousy caused by the valor of the eighty at Thermopylae. An odd reaction.

In A.D. 174, or thereabouts, when Pausanias visited the site, the Lion Gate was visible above the rubble, and many graves, no doubt kept clear by grave robbers, were pointed out. Even these were largely overlaid in time and the memory of them lost in the broiling turbulence of Greek history. Then in 1876, fresh from his triumph at Troy, Schliemann attacked the citadel and within a few weeks was able to telegraph King Paul that he had discovered the tomb of his ancestor.

Of course, since Paul was a Dane, this was not strictly accurate, but the world's debt to Schliemann, for his imagination, his determination, and his luck, remains immeasurable. No one who has seen the Mycenaean room in the National Museum in Athens can be anything but grateful to him. Many have followed where he led the way; treasures are still being found and our knowledge of the past expanded.

Given its story of human sacrifice, cannibalism, murder, incest, rape, and adultery, Mycenae is one place properly approached under a glowering sky, with a darkly melodramatic backdrop provided by Mount Saint Elias, where the last in the chain of beacons sprang into flame to announce the victory at Troy. In full sunlight its initial effect is likely to be anticlimax, though one no sooner rounds the battlement and comes face to face with the Lion Gate than the spell reasserts itself.

One of the incidental pleasures of traveling in Greece is the freemasonry of the road, which supplies the lack of altogether reliable tourist information. Hitchhikers best provide each other with such lore—which Youth Hostel has enough hot water for laundry, what village is not yet surfeited with tourists, where that mad Australian Archie said he was going next—but even more sober citizens learn much this way. The country is so small that every non-Greek one encounters has just come from or is just going to the next place on one's own itinerary, and has valuable advice to exchange. In Andritsena we met a California couple fresh from Mycenae. May this book fall into Paul and Virginia's hands (we do not know their last names), and may they read in it our gratitude for their putting us on to Aristoteles, and thus providing us with one of the most exciting and most enjoyable afternoons we have ever spent anywhere.

Aristoteles is well into his eighties. Schliemann stayed in his father's house during his campaigns at Mycenae, and Aristoteles himself sat on the great man's knee and received candy from his hand. He was bewitched by archaeology and worked under Dorpfeld, Papadimitriou, Wace, Blegen, and the rest. Subsequently he became guardian of the place, a post he held until his retirement, whereupon he relinquished it to his nephew. And recently he has been a guide, both at Mycenae and at Epidauros, where he also worked.

We asked for him at the entrance booth, where his nephew now rules, and were told he was on the citadel. And there we found him, a scarecrow figure in a ragged overcoat despite the blazing sun, tottering about with two couples from Scarsdale. They were about to leave, and we took over.

Aristoteles's first move was to discover your name—your given name, by which he would address you, as you addressed him by his. He found "Zhorzhe" easy enough to handle, but "Lucile" was too much for him and he settled for "Lady" (he has a quite un-Greek deference toward women; so the word had meaning for him).

Whether or not you have the good fortune to meet up with Aristoteles, you should get yourself a guide at Mycenae. The ruins are not labeled, and you will, unless you are a trained archaeologist, find it difficult to follow even the best of the guidebook descriptions. In any event, you will want to see the inner grave circle, where most of Schliemann's finds were made; the Red Bath, where Agamemnon met his doom; the megaron, whose hearth has had to be reburied to protect it from vandals; the ninety-nine-step staircase to the secret cistern; the outer grave circle, discovered only in 1952; and the great tholos (beehive-shaped) tombs known as the Treasury of Atreus, the Tomb of Klytemnestra, and the Tomb of Aigisthos.

The grave circles (now dated around 1600–1500 B.C.) and the tholos tombs (dated from 1500 to 1300 B.C.) provide strong evidence of Egyptian influence, most importantly in the mummification of the dead and the provision of treasure for the life after death. It is also probable that Egypt was the source of the gold—thirty-odd pounds of it—found in the shaft graves, and that it was earned by Mycenaean mercenaries fighting at the side of Egyptians trying to drive out their Hyksos overlords. At the same time that Egyptian influence appears, Minoan (Cretan) influence appears also, and more strongly; one theory is that Minoan ships ferried the mercenaries to and from Egypt.

Minoan influence is in fact so strong that until quite recently it was thought that Mycenae was a

Cretan colony. The quietus to the theory was given by Blegen's discovery at Pylos of hundreds of tablets inscribed in the Linear B that Evans had earlier found in Crete, by Wace's discovery at Mycenae of a few dozen of the same, and by Ventris and Chadwick's demonstration that Linear B was Greek. Linear B being Greek, it follows that if any conquering was done, it was Greeks who conquered Minoans, not the other way around.

If the accepted dates are correct, it is improbable that, unhappily for romance (still, by the way, doggedly clung to by Aristoteles), the tombs so far found had anything to do with the House of Atreus. There are, however, other kinds of romance, and the Treasury of Atreus, whether properly named or not, cannot fail to inspire awe because of its sheer size and perfection, especially when it is remembered that no unsupported ceiling (technically it is not a vault) of equal height and diameter was built in Europe until Hadrian's Roman Pantheon a millennium and a half later. At the time the tomb was built, the ground came about to the level of the massive lintel, said to be the largest cut stone in Europe. The lintel could thus be dragged into place, and its 100-ton weight did not have to be lifted. The upper part of the tomb stood above ground. The stones of the dome were fitted and finished on the inside; outside there were large, roughly triangular gaps, which were packed and smoothed over with small stones and yellow clay, thus rendering it watertight.

Aristoteles provided romance, too. While showing us the outer grave circle, he asked whether we had seen the beautiful little rock-crystal duck in the National Museum. Indeed we had, and it was one of our favorite pieces, to which we had returned again and again. "Zhorzhe and Lady," said Aristoteles, pointing, "I found it there."

Aristoteles could also be affecting. When we asked if we could take his picture, he assented, remarking, "My spirit is all over America." Again, while showing us the Treasury of Atreus, he suggested that the large central chamber was the spirits' meeting place, while the smaller but still sizable side chamber (where the actual burials were) was for the spirits to rest in. "I should like something like this," he said. "A little hole a meter and a half long and a meter and a half deep doesn't give you room to move about."

Every traveler in Greece is, we contend, entitled to produce an archaeological theory or two on his own hook. After all, Schliemann was a military contractor and Ventris an architect, but they confounded the professionals of their days, didn't they? Among our private theories is one concerning the reputedly secret cistern, ninety-nine steps below the walls, which is said to have provided the Mycenaeans with an assured water supply in time of siege.

Aristoteles introduced us to the cistern by sitting on a rock at its entrance and producing two bread-stick-looking objects from a paper bag. At first we thought he was offering us sustenance, but it turned out that the objects were tapers to light our way down the slippery, slimy steps. "Be careful of her, Zhorzhe," he said as he started us on our way. "Always be careful of her." (When you come to Mycenae, remember to bring a strong flashlight. You will want it also in the tholos tombs, and it is a useful supplement to gallantry.)

Well, down we went and are glad we did, for we could not help wondering how secret this secret cistern actually was, particularly in view of the Greeks' tendency throughout history to betray one another out of spite or ambition or on advice of oracle. The water, mind you, was piped from the spring Persieia* far up the hill outside the walls. What would have been easier for a besieging army than to break the pipe or to throw a rotting carcass into the spring?

We wonder whether, if there really was a Dorian invasion, a touching engineer's faith in the efficacy of plumbing may not have led to the final downfall of Mycenae. We point out that pipes from an outside source were also relied on at Pylos and Tiryns, both of which also fell. And there is this negative evidence: on the Athenian Acropolis the Mycenaean spring was within the walls, and Athens is said not to have fallen to the Dorians.

---

* Did we remember to say that Mycenae was founded by Perseus (the same who slew the Gorgon Medusa)? Also that Herakles got the Cyclopes to build the massive walls? Also that Thucydides and others refer to the Dorian invasion as the Return of the Sons of Herakles? Sometimes there are too many things to remember.

Several hundred years later, one may note, the Amphictionic League of Delphi agreed that poisoning a spring or otherwise interfering with a city's water supply was contrary to the rules of land warfare. The rules, needless to say, applied only to wars between members of the league, that is, among friends.

We should like to be able to recommend, in the interest of a clearer impression of the world of Mycenae, a tramp around the six tholos (i.e., beehive-shaped) tombs and numerous chamber tombs that are off the tourist track but still within a mile of the citadel. They are, however, hard to find without a guide (a farmer volunteered his services to George and our son David, happily leaving his wife and mother-in-law to finish harvesting their wheat), the paths are rough, and the burdocks and thistles omnipresent. They would take a half day of your all-too-short time, and the result would still be only a somewhat clearer impression.

As a substitute, you should climb to the highest point of the citadel and look about you, starting with Mount Saint Elias, on the top of which are remains of a Mycenaean lookout post, possibly Klytemnestra's very signal tower. Moving clockwise, one is aware of the spring Persieia in the draw between Mount Saint Elias and Mount Zara. An ancient road wound up and over the saddle and led on to Corinth and to Berbate, where a Late Helladic tholos tomb has been excavated. Another road ran in front of Mount Zara and Mount Aetovouno to the sacred site, 4 miles away, that became the Argive Heraeion, scene of the apotheosis of our friends from Delphi, Kleobis and Biton. Parts of this road, including a causeway, can be seen to the right of the modern road as it makes its last turn toward Mycenae.

Another 5 miles to the southeast are Dendra and Midea, where tholos tombs have yielded rich finds. Then to the south, about 5 miles again, is Tiryns, which is only 3 miles from Nauplia, itself a Mycenaean site. And 5 miles beyond Nauplia, a mile beyond Tolon, stands Asine* rising sheer and lovely from the sea. This site you should visit if you possibly can.

A similar roll could be called starting with Argos, 7 miles slightly to the west of south of Mycenae, and sweeping north past the anciently occupied valleys of the Charandos, the Inachos, and the Kephissos (along which the modern road to Corinth runs) to Mount Saint Elias again. The purpose of this panorama of places seen and places unseen is a comprehension of the established order of the world of Mycenae.

---

* It was here, MacKendrick tells us, that some three million potsherds were found, on the brittle evidence of one of which hangs one of the arguments for an early date (about 1260 *vs.* the traditional date of 1184) for the fall of Troy. None of the sherds is on display at the National Museum in Athens, though no doubt they are all in cellar storerooms, where archaeologists make finds almost as dramatic as those in the field. While preparing to evacuate the museum in 1941, Wace and Marinatos found previously overlooked fragments that enabled them to reconstruct the doorway of the Treasury of Atreus.

Otherwise a hasty tour of the Cyclopean walls here and at Tiryns could lead one to imagine a sparsely settled and constantly embattled land, whereas the Argive Plain has been well populated for at least four thousand years, perhaps more so in the Bronze Age than at any other time before or since.

A moment's thought about the tholos tombs—there are a dozen or more in the neighborhood—reinforces the notion of an established order. For these tombs were no secrets in their own day; as we have seen, most of them extended well above the level of the hillsides into which they were built. Nor could it have been secret that they contained great wealth. That they were built, then, and built outside the citadels, argues that the time and place were relatively peaceful. At the very least, their builders must have been confident that no matter how restive the countryside might become, it was safe from strangers who, worshipping strange gods, might not be in awe of those under whose protection these sacred places stood.

12

THE ARGOLID
AND CORINTH

Drinking the Corinthian sun
Reading the marble ruins
Striding over vineyard seas
ODYSSEUS ELYTIS, *Poems*

Nauplia is the logical center from which to make excursions in the Argolid. Mycenae is only 10 miles away; Tiryns is right beside the road to Argos and Mycenae; Asine is 5 miles to the southeast; Epidauros is about 18 miles away through lovely countryside; Troezen is 30-odd miles farther on. And Nauplia has charms of its own.

Above and behind the town rises the great rock of Palamedi, with its Frankish-Venetian-Turkish fortress. As you breakfast on your balcony you can decide whether the walk up the covered gallery of 857 steps is a challenge to your sporting instincts, or whether you would rather drive up the new road. One goes up for the view, and for the mild excitement of scrambling around dizzying heights amid the ruins of castle halls and dungeons. In spite of its having been used as a prison until recently, and memories of sieges and capitulations, in one of which 11,000 Venetians were beheaded before the tent of the Turkish commander, it is not at all grim in the sunlight.* Palamedes, "the handy man," the legendary hero for whom it is named, was a cheerful type, who is said to have invented some of the letters of the alphabet, arithmetic, the calendar, the lighthouse, and the games of chess and dice. Is Palamedes a folk-memory of the Phoenicians? It would seem so.

Nauplia is a cheerful town, made for strolling. It is pleasant to walk among the lovely but shabby Venetian houses of the main square, to admire the very handsome Venetian building at the end of the square which now houses the museum, to poke among the museum's pottery (including Linear B tablets) and fragments of Mycenaean frescoes for half an hour; and pleasanter still to sit at a table on the quayside in late afternoon, watching the world go by. The scene is lively; people drinking, talking, promenading; a yacht comes in to tie up; fishing boats go out for the night's catch; lights wink on as dusk falls. You feel part of a spectacle, as though the quay were a stage set for a gay opera.

---

* In his book *In Crusader Greece,* Eric Forbes-Boyd speaks of the Venetian lions carved over the entrance gates of Palamedi and the lower fortress of Acronauplia. He calls them "most engaging, with what appear to be long drooping moustaches that give them the air of Edwardian mashers."

As we were sitting there, a discordant note intruded in the joyful harmony. A few feet away there lay a dead dog. Time went by, but no one took any notice. How could people be so callous? We became quite upset. Then miraculously the dead dog arose and walked. Another family joke was born.

TIRYNS (ΤΙΡΥΝΣ)

> The wall is the work of the Cyclopes, made of unwrought stones, each stone being so big that a pair of mules could not move the smallest from its place to the smallest degree.
>
> PAUSANIAS, *Description of Greece*
> (Translation by H. S. Jones)

Tiryns was Herakles' town, at least in some versions of the myth. It was there that he was born, nominally the son of King Amphitryon, but actually the son of Zeus. It was there that he set out to do the twelve labors for his uncle, King Eurystheus.

The citadel rises like a battleship, protecting the flat alluvial plain, in ancient times rich in wheat, now rich in citrus groves and tobacco. Although there is far less mystery and grandeur in the site than at Mycenae, the Cyclopean walls of Tiryns are even more massive. No wonder the ancient Greeks thought that no human hands could have moved these stones, and ascribed the work to the mythical Cyclops. It is awesome to stand in the corbeled casements, whose double walls of immense stones come together overhead in an inverted V.*

In the royal quarters atop the butte you can make out the great court, the megaron, the hearth flanked by four columns, and a great slab of smooth gray stone about ten feet square with a run-off drain, which was the bath. After having stretched your imagination to the breaking point trying to reconstruct the brightly colored pillars and columns, the frescoes of elegant ladies, of warriors and charioteers long since gone, it is very satisfying to see what was without a doubt a bath fit for a king.

EPIDAUROS (ΕΠΙΔΑΥΡΟΣ)

> And all who came Asclepius cured;
> Those whom some taint of nature had laid low,
> And those whose limbs were wounded by the blow
> Of far-flung stone or bronzen-gleaming sword,
> Whom summer suns too fiercely smite
> And whom the freezing winters bite;
> Relieving each peculiar pain,
> And cleansing all from scar and blane.
> And one he healed with spells benign,
> And one with soothing anodyne.
> With simples too their flesh he bound,
> Or with the keen-edged knife restored the festering wound.

PINDAR, *The Third Pythian Ode*
(Translation by C. J. Billson)

* Somewhat similar casements appear, not elsewhere in Greece, but in the Bronze Age *nuraghi* of Sardinia. Corbeled passageways are also found in the Hittite fortifications at Hattusas (Turkey). The Hittites and Mycenaeans were certainly known to each other. If we read Robert Graves's *The White Goddess* aright, there is evidence that (1) among the "Peoples of the Sea" who unsuccess-

Asklepios learned the art of healing from the cen-
taur Chiron, who raised him on the slopes of Mount
Pelion. As the son of Apollo the Healer, he also inherited the ability to make miraculous cures. Pindar
in this same ode recounts the legend of Asklepios'
birth. Apollo had visited the princess Koronis and
left her with child. Without her father's knowledge
and without waiting for the marriage rites, she took
another lover, and what was worse, a stranger.

> *For she like many others held most dear*
> *What lay beyond her own familiar ways,*
> *As mortals oft who scorn their homely sphere*
> *On things far distant bend a foolish gaze,*
> *Pursuing idle dreams and hopes unsatisfied.*

Poor child, with her idle dreams! Perhaps she felt
abandoned by the god, and could look forward only
to being a pawn in a dynastic marriage, as is the lot
of princesses. So she fell in love with a handsome
stranger, and paid with her life, for Apollo in his
jealousy sent his sister Artemis to kill Koronis. But
he snatched the baby Asklepios from the funeral pyre
and conveyed him to Chiron.

Asklepios' death was also the work of the gods. He
had restored so many of the dead to life that Hades

---

fully attacked Egypt around 1200 B.C. were Hittites, Mycenaeans,
and Sherdina, and (2) the Sherdina gave their name to Sardinia.
From all this it is perhaps safe to conclude merely, again, that the
ancient world was more tightly knit than our freshman history
survey course dreamed of.

complained, and Zeus with his thunderbolt slew Asklepios, who was then deified.

By the fourth century the cult of Asklepios was enormously popular at Epidauros and had supplanted that of Apollo. There were many other Greek Asklepeions, notably at Kos and Pergamon. Asklepios' daughters Panacaea and Hygeia were also the objects of a cult.

The sanctuary of Asklepios at Epidauros contained a temple for the worship of the god, a gymnasium, palaestra, and stadium, hostels for pilgrims, and a dormitory where the sick lay to be visited by the god in their dreams. The priests then interpreted these dreams and suggested a treatment. The element of faith healing as at Lourdes or Tinos today was strong, but practical remedies, the healing power of water in fountains and baths as in a nineteenth-century spa, and the power of suggestion were mixed in proportions that cannot now be determined, nor can the role of the sacred snakes be assessed. Excavators have found inscriptions recording forty-three miraculous cures.

One of the curiosities of Epidauros is a small circular building (tholos) whose foundations alone are visible. Below ground level these foundations are divided by three walls in concentric rings to form a maze. Here perhaps the sacred snakes were kept and worshipped. In the fourth century Polykleitos the Younger, a sculptor and architect from Argos, built a round temple here. It must have been one of the most sumptuous and beautiful buildings ever built. In the museum on the grounds, sections of this tholos have been reconstructed, the marble fragments found at the site being supplemented by plaster. The floor was laid in black-and-white marquetry, the columns and ceiling were decorated with flowers of acanthus and hibiscus exquisitely carved. Do not shun this museum. It is far more interesting than the ruins themselves, except for the theater, which is also attributed to Polykleitos.

Every four years a festival in honor of Asklepios was held, with athletic games and contests of music, poetry, and drama. For this purpose the theater was built in the fourth century. Today it is the best-preserved ancient theater in Greece, and the only one to have a circular orchestra in Greek style (in most others the Romans walled in the orchestra, made it watertight, and used it for aquatic shows and miniature naval battles). The Greeks built their theaters to please the eye as well as the ear. The curving rows of seats are cut into a natural hillside, and Greece being Greece, there is always a view of the hills near or far.

The proper way to see a theater is in action. A festival of Classical drama is presented each year at Epidauros from mid-June to mid-July. To see a presentation of one of the plays of Aeschylus, Sophokles, Euripides, or Aristophanes in this sanctuary of the god of healing must bring forcibly to mind the difference between the Greek and the Roman ways. The Romans had their theaters too, and their dramatists, but their largest assemblies of people were for the gladiatorial contests in the arenas, not for the Greek drama's public inquiry into the human mind and soul.

The acoustics of this theater are so nearly perfect that every word can be heard in every seat. Visitors today love to test this engineering feat. They stand in the center of the orchestra on a stone that once held the altar where sacrifices to Dionysios were made. There they strike a match, drop a coin, declaim a verse, or sing. When we walked up to the theater, whom should we hear singing but our Dutch hitchhiking friend, Siwart, to whom we had said good-bye the previous evening.

We gave him a ride back almost to Nauplia, where our road branched off to Tolon, a pretty fishing village on a sandy bay. Tolon is a most agreeable place to have a simple lunch and a swim. From this little beach, as from many others large and small, the British Expeditionary Force in the last days of May, 1941, took off little groups of soldiers who were soon to make another stand and endure another defeat on Crete.

As we were leaving Tolon who should come walking up the beach but Finn, our Danish friend, who had been to nearby Asine to see the Mycenaean ruins. We had also said our good-byes to him the day before.

Did these boys have extrasensory perception? It was uncanny but pleasant to see Finn again; we gave him a ride all the way to Athens and said good-bye on the pier at Piraeus. A week later, in the Sultan's palace in Istanbul, there was Finn. It was a happy reunion, but this time we had no car, and it was really good-bye. These boys, who had finished their education and their military service, were having a *Wanderjahr* in the old European tradition before settling down to the serious business of earning a living. It was always a pleasure to see one or the other of them popping up on our path, and to share their enthusiasm for the road.

TROEZEN (TPOIZHN)

> *Theseus' mother Aethra, conducting him to the stone, and informing him who was his true father, commanded him to take from thence the tokens that Aegeus had left, and sail to Athens. He without any difficulty set himself to the stone and lifted it up, but refused to take the journey by sea, though it was much the safer way.*
> PLUTARCH, *Theseus*
> (Translation by John Dryden)

As we shall have other occasions to remark, there is no accurate road map of Greece that we know of. It is likely that the one you have shows Troezen, if at all, as though it were isolated from Nauplia. Yet in Nauplia you can get a bus for Poros (what is meant is Galata across the strait), and from Galata you can get a taxi to Troezen. A better plan, if you take a taxi or your own car to Epidauros, is to continue on to Troezen from there, traveling on the admittedly primitive roads that are there even though the map knows them not. The two places can be readily done in a day.

Troezen is perhaps best left for your second trip, and yet we and some friends enjoyed it immensely. It is an Adventure, and it is one even your well-traveled friends are not likely to have experienced: *you* can be *first*. It is unspoiled: the only other tourists you will see there are other readers of this book. And of course the site is rich in legend and the scenery delightful.

Your taxi will get you only as far as the modern village of Troezena, where at the first taverna on the left beyond the little modern monument you can persuade the proprietor, Boutsiphakos Athanasios, to guide you. His English is rudimentary but his goodwill is boundless. He may want to lead you on the most direct route, fording a brook and brushing stoically ahead through thistles and briars. There is a slightly longer route following cart tracks and easily negotiable paths. It would be nice if your Greek were good enough to tell him that that is the way you want to go. Otherwise you had better wear slacks for the expedition. And the sun will be hot.

But you will be rewarded with a view of the sacred

stone Theseus lifted, or so it is said. And the acropolis where stood his grandfather's palace, where he was born and brought up. And the spot, now marked by the ruins of a Byzantine church, where Phaedra watched Hippolytos at his gymnastics and conceived her fatal passion. And the shore where the sea monster caused Hippolytos' horses to drag him to his death. Theseus may have been a real person as well as a mythological hero; Troezen was certainly a real city. Many Athenian women and children took refuge there in 480 B.C. during the Persian occupation of Athens.

The whole Theseus story has been attractively told by Mary Renault in *The King Must Die* and *The Bull from the Sea* in a way that makes the strange customs of prehistoric times understandable to modern minds. We have lost touch with the primitive world where gods and goddesses determine a man's fate.

However much we puzzle over Euripides' *Hippolytos*, we cannot shake off the notion that the great sin, the moral lapse of the play, is Phaedra's, when in her suicide letter she falsely accuses Hippolytos of seducing her. But to the Greeks this was hardly more than an incident in the plot and seems to have been common enough in the ancient world, *vide* Potiphar's wife, the thirteenth-century (B.C.) Egyptian "Tale of the Two Brothers," and the Homeric account of Bellerophon and Anteia. In the American South today false accusations of rape are not unheard of. To the

Greeks it was Hippolytos' hubris in refusing to worship Aphrodite which caused the tragedy. Perhaps it would help to see the play staged in the Greek manner. Certainly Marie Bell's production of Racine's *Phèdre* does very little to make one feel as the Greeks felt, or even as the French of the time of Louis XIV. The religious and dynastic problems seem remote. And Eugene O'Neill's attempt in *Desire Under the Elms* to rewrite the Theseus-Phaedra-Hippolytos story is just a trifle sophomoric. In the end we turn back to Euripides, to what is human in the play—the grief-stricken father who has wrongfully caused the death of his son. The last scene of *Hippolytos,* when Theseus takes the dying Hippolytos in his arms, is one of the great reconciliation scenes of all literature.

CORINTH (ΚΟΡΙΝΘΟΣ)

> Not for every man the trip to Corinth.
> Greek Proverb

Corinth was the city of commerce and pleasure, where one thousand temple prostitutes, slave girls in the service of Aphrodite, made the secular sacred. The most renowned and expensive of Corinthian ladies of love was Lais, who entertained philosophers and princes, although it is recorded that Demosthenes found her price too high and did not buy. Robert Liddell in his delightful book *The Morea* tells of another suitor who met with coldness. "He, however,

attributed the cause of his ill reception to the whiteness of his hair, and dyed it a brown color, but to no
purpose; 'Fool that thou art,' said the courtesan, 'to
ask today what I refused yesterday to thy father.' "

It was in this same city four hundred years later
that St. Paul lived and preached and wrote his letters
to the Thessalonians and the Romans.

Among the legendary rulers of Corinth were Si-
syphos; his grandson Bellerophon, who captured the
winged horse, Pegasos; and Jason and Medea. The
Corinthian legends naturally told a different story
about Medea from the one we know through the
Athenian playwright Euripides. They made her com-
partively innocent, not a child-murderer at all, though
even in Corinth there was a story involving a poisoned
robe which Medea sent to Glauke, her successor in
Jason's love. Pausanias saw the tomb of Medea's children, which was shown to visitors as late as the second century A.D.; but visitors today have to be content
to know that it was near the Odeon and the Fountain
of Glauke.

Corinth is rich in history and rich in ruins. The
noblest of these is the Temple of Apollo, whose seven
remaining columns of yellow limestone, monolithic,
a little heavy, show the strength that is always present
in the beginnings of a style, especially a strong style
like the Doric. In the early sixth century, Corinth,
under the firm hand of the tyrant Periander, set the
fashion in pottery and architecture. The triangular

pediment is said to be a Corinthian innovation. Unfortunately, the pediment of the Temple of Apollo is long since gone, nor is any contemporary description left to us. The whole city was razed by the Romans in 146 B.C. and the only eyewitness accounts of Corinth date from after the devastation of the city. One hundred years later Corinth was recolonized by order of Julius Caesar. Another city grew, received Nero, St. Paul, Hadrian, and (who else?) Herodes Atticus. It too fell to the Goths and the earthquakes. Archaeologists have uncovered the remains, mostly Roman, of eight temples, three theaters, five springs (the great limestone rock called Acrocorinth supplied plenty of pure water), five markets, five hot baths, a gymnasium, an asklepeion, several mosaics, a potters' quarter, and the ancient walls which protected the city and its access to the port of Lechaion.

There is more than enough to see at Corinth without climbing the Acrocorinth, but those who take the time to go up will be rewarded by a view which encompasses the mountains of Arcadia, the Corinthian and Saronic Gulfs, the heights of Parnassos and Helikon, and on clear days, the Acropolis of Athens. Armchair travelers might read the chapter on Corinth in Kathleen Freeman's *Greek City-States*, full of cloak-and-dagger stories about Corinth and Acrocorinth—true stories, originally told by Plutarch. Venetians, Franks, Byzantines, and Turks later fought and tricked each other to gain possession of this natural key to the Peloponnesos.

Leaving Corinth for Athens you go through the dull modern town, which suffered terribly from an earthquake in 1928. Soon you pass the turnoff to the ancient Sanctuary of Isthmia, whose games and victorious athletes were celebrated by Pindar. Near this spot on the Isthmus in 1306 there took place a grand tournament at the invitation of the Prince of Achaea. One thousand knights contested in their heavy armor under the hot sun; surely one of the strangest, literally outlandish events ever to occur on Greek soil.

13

MYKONOS

ΜΥΚΟΝΟΣ

The Isles of Greece

What are the islands to me,
What is Greece?

What is Naxos, Paros, Milos,
What is the circle about Lycia,
What, the Cyclades'
White necklace?

What is Naxos, Tinos, Andros,
and Delos, the clasp
of the white necklace?

What are the islands to me,
What is Greece?

H.D., *The Islands*

The Venus de Milo, the Woman of Andros, the Naxian lions, Parian marble—we all have associations with these islands of the Cyclades. It would be pleasant to seek each one out and sample its special quality, but for those who have only a short vacation to spend in Greece, the Cyclades will usually mean Mykonos and Delos.

Visiting the Cyclades in May, June, or September is preferable to a trip in July or August, when a strong north wind called the *meltémi* blows and makes the sea rough. But thousands enjoy Mykonos in July and August, and if you must go then, go—with reservations and dramamine. Tourist-watching, a great sport, will be at its height. Ladies in large straw hats will be painting their everlasting watercolors; the pink pelicans will be performing by the fountain at the

harbor; fishermen will be mending nets; the sea will
be brilliant blue, green, and violet; and the white-
washed houses of the town will seem blindingly white
in the sun as they cast welcome shade on the little
streets wide enough only for a donkey. One of the
joys of Mykonos is wandering along these winding
streets, savoring the rightness of the cubistic architecture (which influenced Le Corbusier, and through
him all modern building)—the purity of line, the
purity of color, whitewash everywhere, even on the
pavements, with doors and windowframes in red or
blue for accent, and more color in great pots of pink
oleanders and scarlet hibiscus or deep-green vines,
all this set against a stark background of stony-brown
earth and rock, with hardly a tree. Windmills on the
skyline serve as relief instead.

Most of the windmills on Mykonos are quiet now,
but one is still working on a rise near the Hotel Xenia,
and the miller will be happy to show you how he
grinds the grain and to sell you a postcard, too. But
this commercialization is not offensive. He is really
friendly, neither servile nor pushy. By some miracle
the Greeks, expecially the Mykoniats, have kept both
their habit of friendliness and their innate dignity
while being overrun by thousands of tourists. Certainly they like the money; they appreciate what
tourism has done for them economically; but there is
very little of the resentment of the tourist for having
changed their way of life that one sometimes meets

elsewhere. We have found the shopkeepers (and Mykonos has countless shops selling hand-knit sweaters and handwoven bags, blouses, shirts, and skirts) all pleasant to deal with, friendly beyond the line of duty, giving us a present of a string of "worry beads"* or offering us chocolates when we made a small purchase.

In fact, Mykonos is a good place to buy a few of those indispensable gifts to take home. The handwoven textiles are not expensive, their color and design are very attractive; but the cut of the garments is rather foursquare and the sizes only approximate. So don't go overboard; choose with care. You can buy the woven fabric as piece goods; you can settle for articles where fit is not important, or if you wish, you may seek out the smarter shops along the "main" street which runs perpendicular to the waterfront, where high-style sportswear can be found. But Mykonos is not Miami, nor even Capri, thank goodness, and much of its appeal lies in its simplicity and directness. You can look in, or step in, through an open doorway and see a girl at work on her loom, surrounded by hanks of hand-dyed wool.

Mykonos has a lively night life, of the most informal kind. Indeed, everything is informal on this holiday island. There are many paths to ramble on between stone walls looking over stony fields with the

---

* These beads are constantly twirled by Greek men, as Americans jingle their change.

sea in the distance and several good beaches with fine white sand. Also with a fine assortment of plastic squeeze bottles in all colors. At the rate things are going, the Aegean will be armpit deep in squeeze bottles in another ten years. Since, like potsherds, they are immortal, one can imagine the archaeologists of the future conducting colloquia on the Squeeze Bottle Folk, and bitterly disputing whether the Blue Bottle Folk conquered the Frosty-Pink Bottle Folk or the other way around.

There are said to be 365 chapels on Mykonos, erected as thanksgiving offerings by fishermen or sailors home safe from the sea. Piracy was endemic in the Aegean in the eighteenth and the early nineteenth century, and some of these seamen were certainly pirates. Yet, with their counterparts from Hydra and Spetsai, they formed the navy which helped to liberate Greece from the Turks in 1821, and Mykonos is proud of the part it played in the War of Independence. Some of these chapels are tiny, used only by one family. All are sparkling white and tended with devotion; all are photogenic, expecially the Paraportiani, near the post office, with its domes and cubes and stepped gables. Mykonos is made to order for camera or paintbox.

There are approximately thirteen sailings a week from Piraeus to Mykonos. The trip takes from six to eleven hours depending on what stops are made. During the first hour or so you will have the coast of Attica

on your left (port) side. Soon after the Acropolis and
Mount Lykabettos fade from sight, you can start looking for Poseidon's temple on its headland at Sounion,
and only after it sinks below the horizon do you begin
to entertain yourself by watching the other passengers. We were offered a chance, which we were not
sporting enough to take, of winning a string of red
mullet in a raffle.

Henry Miller, in *The Colossus of Maroussi*, describes a trip in Greek waters:

The wind was up and the boat was pitching and tossing. Some of the roughest seas in this part of the Mediterranean. Good seas. Fine rough weather, man-sized,
appetizing. A little boat in a big sea. An island now and
then. A tiny harbor lit up like a Japanese fairy tale.
Animals coming aboard, children screaming, food cook-
ing, men and women washing up in the hold at a little
trough, like animals. Fine boat, fine weather. Stars now
and then soft as geraniums, or hard and splintery like
riven pikes. Homely men walking about in carpet slippers, playing with their beads, spitting, belching, making
friendly grimaces, tossing their heads back and with a
clicking noise saying no when they should be saying yes.*
In the rear of the boat the steerage passengers, sprawled
pell-mell over the deck, their possessions spread out
around them, some snoozing, some coughing, some singing, some meditating, some arguing, but whether asleep
or awake all joined indiscriminately one to another and
giving an impression of life. Not that sterile, sickly,

* Our note: The Greek word *naí* (pronounced NAY) means "yes."

organized life of the tourist third class such as we know on the big ocean liners, but a contaminating, infectious, pullulating, bee-hive life such as human beings ought to share when they are making a perilous voyage over a great body of water.

We may not all want to drink in life in such big gulps. You can buy a first-class or second-class passage, with or without cabin, or a deck passage, depending on your purse and on the weather. It can be very pleasant under the stars of a summer evening, or it can be cold and rough, with many seasick passengers, and you might be glad to "seek the seclusion that your cabin grants." Our daughter made this trip one August, and because of the crowds took refuge in a lifeboat, where she made the acquaintance of some French students who are still her friends, and are referred to in the family as "those kids from the lifeboat."

Whatever you choose, remember that it is colder on the water. Bring a sweater or a jacket along, but, if you are returning to Athens, pack lightly in a small suitcase for this trip, leaving your main baggage at your Athens hotel. You will alight at Mykonos not on a wharf but in a small launch, and the less baggage the better for this little feat. This is nothing to be alarmed about; but, just the same, there is no reason to bring your city clothes to Mykonos.

14

DELOS

ΔΗΛΟΣ

But Delos is pleasant, O Phoebus, above the rest.
Long-robed Ionians there gather in to thy feast
with children and gentle wives, a holiday throng
who look to thy pleasure in boxing and dance and song,
and ever, when games are appointed, make trial of skill
remembering thee, and the joy of thy heart fulfil.
                              Homeric Hymn to Apollo,
                              (Translation by T. F. Higham)

Deprived of its pomp and bustle, its port sanded up, Delos is now usually reached from Mykonos. The caïque (fare, 16 drachmas round trip) leaves Mykonos around nine o'clock each morning. As soon as it is well filled up, the lady engineer disappears below to her engines, and after a leisurely chug of forty-five minutes, you alight at Delos and run the gamut of souvenir vendors. At one o'clock the caïque returns, so you will have only three hours at your disposal on Delos. The unusually serious traveler may try to reserve in advance one of the eight beds in the tourist pavilion, the only accommodation on the island, or he may hire a boat on Mykonos for his own party. The very best way, of course, is to arrive at Delos on your own yacht, which you have chartered with a group of friends, and after the caïque leaves have Delos all to yourself, to see the sunset from Mount Kynthos, to walk among the ruins by moonlight (though the guard will chase you if you stray far from the harbor). But for most of us, three hours will have to suffice.

It takes a generous supply of imagination to roll back twenty-seven or more centuries and transform in the mind's eye this small, bare island—"windy and waste and battered by the sea," in Kallimachos' words; treeless, waterless, covered with ruins—into the religious, social, and commercial metropolis that Delos was in the ancient world.

Delos was settled by Mycenaean times, as recent excavations of palace, temples, and houses prove. It was here that Theseus composed and danced the crane dance, as tradition says and readers of *The King Must Die* will remember. In the seventh century, when the unknown poet wrote the Homeric Hymn we quote, Delos had, by reason of its central location in the Ionian Sea and because tradition made it the birthplace of Apollo and Artemis, taken its place with Delphi and Olympia as one of the three great Panhellenic sanctuaries, where religious ceremonies involving sacrifices, processions, games, and banquets attracted pilgrims and traders. Myth has it that Leto, pregnant because of dalliance with her brother Zeus, was pursued from place to place by jealous Hera's serpent, and finally found refuge on poor, barren Delos, tempting the Delians with a picture of the glory and economic advantage that would accrue to the island as the birthplace of the divine twins. After nine days and nights of labor she gave birth, while holding on to the sacred palm tree, first to Artemis, then to Apollo, who immediately called for his bow and his lyre.

So Delos became the site of the cult of Apollo Lyceus (gleaming Apollo? or wolfish Apollo? or Apollo from Lycia, a reference to the Asiatic origin of the god?). At any rate, his sacred island gleamed with marble temples—several for himself; one for his mother, Leto; one for his sister, Artemis; and many others. Ranged along the terrace by the sacred lake were the famous Naxian lions, so often photographed. Naxos, a neighboring island rich in marble, was master of Delos in the seventh and sixth centuries before Athens moved in, and Naxian sculptors carved these curious, noble, elongated beasts, unlike any lions they probably never saw, with a lean and hungry look, and a hint of Egypt in them.

The loveliest manifestation of archaic art left to us on Delos are the *kouroi* and the *korai* in the little museum. We have seen these vigorous youths and delicate maidens in Athens in the Acropolis Museum and in the National Archaeological Museum. The boys have a look of the time when the world was young, but the girls are all Ionian grace and refinement, with their ringleted hair, their painted necklaces, and their pleated mantles of fine linen. The superb technique of the sculptor makes the marble seem like gossamer.

As the center of the Delian League, a place of pilgrimage and busy port, Delos grew so rich that Athens cast a covetous eye, and as the strong will do, moved in to "protect" it. Twice in the fifth century B.C. Athens declared a "purification" of the island, removing the contents of all the sacred tombs to the nearby island of Rheneia, and forbidding birth or death to take place on Delos. This seeming contravention of nature was accomplished by sending those about to do either to Rheneia. There must have been some slip-ups. One wonders how they were dealt with.

Of more historical import, as Athens transformed the Delian League into an Athenian empire, sometimes by harsh or even foul means (in 422 and again in 166 the entire population of Delos was removed by order of Athens), she took over the administration of the shrines, removed the funds of the league (contents of the treasuries) to Athens for safekeeping, and used the revenues not only to build up her fleet but to rebuild the Acropolis after the Persians sacked it. Some of the tribute that had formerly enriched Delian Apollo went to glorify the Parthenon of the goddess Athena. This can hardly be a matter of regret to us now, but we can regret that, although Perikles proposed a Panhellenic Congress in 449 to solve the common problems of the Greek states, it was never held; the confederation never evolved into a federation; and the Athenian empire which usurped its place also failed to create Greek unity.

In 376 Delos revolted against Athens, but the revolt was easily suppressed. Around 315, after Athens'
defeat by Philip II of Macedon, Delos became inde-
pendent and waxed richer than ever on trade, especially in grain, being safe from pirates because it was
sacred soil. During Hellenistic and Roman times, more
and more temples, porticos, statues, marketplaces,
merchants' clubs and mansions, docks, and warehouses
were built. The population of the island grew to 100,-
000 under the Romans, says Paul MacKendrick. Thousands of slaves changed hands there in a year, or
even in a day (10,000 in one day, again according to
MacKendrick). The secular outstripped the sacred,
although many gods were worshipped. Traders from
Alexandria, Beirut, and Tyre brought their own gods
—Isis, Serapis, Atargartis, whose licentious cult
alarmed the Athenians. This cosmopolitan city became the greatest trading center of the Aegean; when
the Romans made it a free port in 166 B.C., Rhodes
was ruined. But it was sacked in A.D. 88 by Mithra-
dates, an Asia Minor prince who was warring against
Rome, and repeatedly thereafter it was looted by
pirates, until only the stone robbers disturbed the
ruins. In 1873 the French School of Athens began
excavations which still continue.

Remember to carry your guidebook so as not to
wander aimlessly among the ruins. Map in hand, sun-
shade on head, start with the easy ascent of Mount
Kynthos. You will pass on the way a Roman house of

considerable luxury called the House of Hermes, with two stories standing, an atrium, and a cistern. All over Delos are remains of ancient cisterns partially filled with water and with frogs that know their Aristophanes and keep repeating "Brekekekex ko-ax!" Your path will then take you along the Terrace of the Alien Gods, where the Temple of Isis, whose façade has been re-erected, stands as the most beautiful of the ruins left on Delos. You will also pass a sacred cave, and near the summit the sites of the temples of Zeus and Athena Kynthos. There is a first-century mosaic inscription at the summit, but the purpose of the climb is the view. From this little pinnacle, 365 feet high, you can see the Cyclades ranged all around (*Kyklos* means "circle"), their blue hills rising from the blue sea—Tinos, Mykonos, Naxos, Paros, Siphnos, Seriphos, Kithnos, Syros. It becomes apparent why Delos was called the navel of the Aegean, a chosen place, the source of the light of Apollo.

On the descent, turn left at the Terrace of the Alien Gods to reach the House of the Dolphins and the House of the Masks, so called after the beautiful mosaic floors of these rich merchants' dwellings. Delos is sometimes compared to Pompeii on the strength of these houses, but the comparison is misleading. In life, Delos was incomparably more important than Pompeii, which after all was not much more than a summer resort or a wealthy suburb. But as a ruin, at least as a Roman ruin, Delos is much inferior, al-

though it is an archaeologist's dream. In short, there
are no wall paintings. The irony of it is that the greatest of the mosaics at Pompeii were created by Greeks,
while the mosaics on Delos are thought to be by
Syrian artists. Be that as it may, the mosaics, especially that of Dionysios on his panther in the House
of the Masks and the emblem of life in the House of
the Dolphins, are lovely, though a bit dimmer than
they appear on the postcards. (They are photographed
for this purpose while wet.)

The theater need not take your time; you will have
seen other more impressive theaters in Greece. But
just below the theater is the House of the Trident
with more mosaics, and the House of Dionysios, with
another mosaic of the god riding on a panther.

The rest of your visit can be devoted to a stroll
through the acres of marble to the Terrace of the
Lions and the Sacred Lake, now dry, making as much
as you can of the very ruined ruins, and saving some
time for the small but very interesting museum. There
may even be ten minutes left for dabbling your feet
by the sandy shore of the ancient Sacred Port, where
pieces of marble and pottery lie in the shallow water,
to be had for the taking, at the spot where once the
"holiday throng" stepped ashore to pay homage to
Apollo.

15

ISLAND
EXTRAS

Where grew the arts of war and peace.
BYRON, *Don Juan*

An aspect of the human condition is that any place easy to get to is soon spoiled. This is a solemn thought the ancient Greeks would have appreciated. It is illustrated today by the islands of the Aegean: for the most part they are neither too easy to get to nor too much spoiled. With an extra week or so, and close, on-the-spot study of steamer and plane schedules, you can make a reasonably good sampling of their pleasures.

SAMOS (ΣΑΜΟΣ)

Samos is a large island, mountainous, wooded with pines, bright with flowers, fertile with olives and the vineyards that have made Samian wine a byword since ancient times. It is easy to see why Antony and

Cleopatra chose Samos as a place of rest and revelry. Every prospect pleases, whether one looks to the mountains of the interior, or from the courtyard of a monastery toward the sea below and across the narrow strait at the high blue outline of Cape Mykale in Turkey. This strait, only a mile and a quarter wide, was the scene of a famous naval battle in 479 B.C. when the Ionian cities rose in revolt against the Persians and defeated their fleet. It was on this same day, according to tradition, that the land Battle of Plataea was fought and won, thus ending the Persian Wars.

The great days of Samos were early and were mostly the work of the tyrant Polykrates. In his time (the latter half of the sixth century B.C.), the Temple of Hera was built, the largest Greek temple ever built; only a solitary cockeyed column now stands. He protected his harbor with a tremendous mole, whose foundations can still be seen at Tigani. And he (or perhaps his father) performed a typically Greek miracle in driving a tunnel almost a mile through a mountain.

The miracle was typical in that it is an example of first-rate primitive engineering, that it cost the lives of thousands of slaves over a fifteen-year period, and that it was quite unnecessary. Water could have been brought around the mountain as safely as through it —and of course far more easily. It is no longer possible to go completely through the tunnel, but you can penetrate far enough to bring out whatever claustrophobia is in you. Don't forget your flashlight.

The career of Polykrates provides Herodotos with a complement to the tale of Kleobis and Biton. For Polykrates had too much good fortune. He knew it, and so feared a terrible end. Hoping to avoid his fate, he took his most valuable ring, of which he was very fond, and threw it into the sea. But it was not easy for him to bring himself bad luck: a fisherman found the ring in the stomach of one of his catch and reverently presented it to the tyrant, who then knew he was in for it. Indeed he was. Shortly thereafter he was tricked into visiting the Persian satrap across the strait; there he was treacherously seized and flayed alive, proving again to Herodotos that no man can call himself happy until his end.

PATMOS (ΠΑΤΜΟΣ)

Patmos is the northernmost of the Dodekanese, a group of twelve islands in the southern Aegean near the coast of Turkey. (δοδεκα means "twelve," and νισοι, pronounced NISI, means "islands.") Brown and bare because of the volcanic nature of the rock, Patmos has a pleasant white harbor town with a large central square, but it is visited chiefly for the monastery of St. John the Divine, which lies on the ridge above. Here, according to tradition, St. John dictated the apocalyptic vision that we know as The Revelation of St. John. "I John," he wrote (1:9), "who also am your brother, and companion in tribulation, and in the kingdom and patience of Jesus Christ, was in the isle that is called Patmos, for the word of God, and for the testimony of Jesus Christ."

Visitors are shown the grotto where St. John purportedly lived and the rock upon which his disciple Prochoros rested his papyrus while he wrote.

The monastery also has a collection of ancient manuscripts, including thirty-three leaves of the Gospel of St. Mark in the fifth-century Codex Porphyrius. Other leaves of this beautiful manuscript written in silver on purple vellum are in the Bodleian Library at Oxford, in the Vatican, and in Leningrad.

KOS (ΚΟΣ)

In many ways Kos resembles Rhodes on a smaller scale; the same soft air and semitropical vegetation, harbor fortifications built by the Knights of St. John, and minarets left from the Turkish occupation. But Kos has something unique—the great Asklepeion, where medicine was practiced and taught among the temples and the altars and the healing springs. The three long terraces connected by great flights of marble steps make a grand sight, their horizontal lines broken by ruined columns and that most statuesque of tree forms, the cypress. The Asklepeion lies about 2 miles outside the town, an easy expedition. No scrambling among rocks or up steep mountainsides, although the mountains of Kos lie behind the sanctuary, and across the narrow sea below, the mountains of Anatolian Turkey. The remains we see are Hellenistic with some Roman additions, the product of an urbane civilization whose spirit is expressed in the *Idylls* of Theokritos, who lived and wrote on Kos.

But the great spirit hovering over the island is that of Hippokrates. "The plane tree of Hippokrates" stands in the town square, although it is certain that Hippokrates never saw that particular tree. No matter. And no matter that the Hippokratic oath in its present form dates from a later time than the fifth century B.C. when he lived. In the third century scholars from Alexandria found a body of manuscripts in the medical school of the Asklepeion. These writings, by Hippokrates and his successors, are known as the Hippokratic treatises, and form one of the great legacies of the Greeks to the Western world. Other ancient civilizations had physicians, such as the doctors of the Pharaohs, who made accurate and subtle observations on disease. But medicine did not become a science until the Ionian natural philosophers led men to think of nature as a whole, with man at the hub, using the power of his reason to find universal laws.

Of all the islands we so blithely label "Extras," Samos and Kos are the ones most recommended.

SANTORINI (ΘHPA)

The name Santorini or Santorin comes from the Italian for St. Irene, the patron saint of the island. It was known in Classical times as Thera, and that name is also used again today. You have probably seen, on travel posters or in ads put out by the Greek National Tourist Office, pictures of the harbor framed in a circle of bare peaks, the deep blue-green waters filling the crater of an ancient volcano (which cannot be called extinct but merely quiescent for the moment), the great multi-colored cliff with the broad white steps zigzagging up to the dazzling white town laid like a chaplet along the ridge. You may have read May Sarton's novella *Joanna and Ulysses* about the pathetic little waif donkey saved by the lonely girl painter. In fact, you may be fortunate enough to have Joanna as your guide in Greece, for Joanna turns out to be a real and fascinating person who not only paints but acts as a tourist guide. She can be reached through the agency "Hermès en Grèce."

You may also have read in Robert Payne's *The Isles of Greece* of the author's dangerous journey on muleback up those 800 zigzag steps on Santorini. You may want to emulate such a brave exploit. Thousands of people do, every year, and once on top they look over the other edge to see a gentle slope down to the sea a mile away. No good telling yourself that there is no harbor on that side of the island for the big ships to anchor in. That gentle slope takes all the drama out of the mule ride and leaves one feeling rather foolish. And it is no good, if you are by nature timid, or allergic to donkeys, to decide to cast false pride to the winds and walk up the steps. You will find yourself ankle deep in donkey dung on a hot day.

Santorini has some antiquities, but few that are unique. All the interest of the island is in its exotic setting; all the beauty of the island is in those striking photographs so often reproduced. Keep your dreams, and save your time for some other enchanted island.

IOS (ΙΟΣ), SERIPHOS (ΣΕΡΙΦΟΣ), SIPHNOS (ΣΙΦΝΟΣ)

A small landlocked harbor, a domed white chapel on a promontory, a white town on a hill, a few cafés by the waterfront, a sandy beach curving off to right or left, farmers and fishermen going about their work: any one of these islands is a delight to see, a picture to keep in the mind and bring out on cold rainy days, with memories of a sail or a swim in the clear, bouyant water.

There is no tourist industry here. Anyone going to these islands to stay must be motivated by a desire for peace and quiet, and fortified by a strong sense of self-sufficiency and the ability to adapt to the peasant way of life. We know an American couple who lived happily on Siphnos for several months; the young bride baked bread in the village oven and washed clothes with the village women. But on Ios we met a scragglybearded expatriate who came aboard our boat ostensibly to ask us about a disease attacking his chickens. His novel wasn't going very well either. We thought his wife looked forlorn, pushing the baby carriage over the cobblestones on the quay. Nor did he bring her aboard with him to taste some contact with the world of home.

In antiquity the gold mines of Siphnos produced such wealth that in the sixth century B.C. the little island was able to build a treasury along the Sacred Way at Delphi. Fragments from the frieze of the Siphnian Treasury are now among the treasures of the Delphi Museum. Ios is reputed to be the place where Homer died. Seriphos has no such claims to past glory. It is just itself, the most beautiful of these little islands.

PAROS (ΠΑΡΟΣ)

Paros is a pleasant island with a pretty town of white houses and winding lanes characteristic of the Cyclades. It is not so crowded as Mykonos, nor so remote as to be devoid of tourist accommodations. There is an excellent beach in the lovely cove of Naoussa, some distance by local bus from the town.

Paros has no special distinction now beyond its beauty. The famous quarries which once produced the fine-grained white marble that took a satin sheen under the hand of ancient sculptors are no longer worked for export. Modern economics mitigates against the excellent.

The church of the Ekatontapyliani (freely, The

Hundred Doors, but exactly what that means, we have no idea), is said to be the finest church in the Aegean. It is of considerable interest, with a dome on pendentives, a handsome stone choir screen, and a sixth-century baptismal font, but one should not expect to find a Mont St. Michel in the Aegean.

One of the curiosities in the town is a mediaeval tower built of ancient marble columns. As Ernle Bradford says: "Tucked in between carved blocks of marble, the old columns protrude like giant cotton reels."

NAXOS (ΝΑΞΟΣ)

Everyone agrees that Naxos is the largest of the Cyclades and one of the most lush (a relative judgment), and that the town of Naxia is a poor thing moderately endowed with Venetian memorabilia; we have no reason to interpose a demurrer.

The town, however, is alleged to have a museum. We know of it only by hearsay. It is not mentioned by the guidebooks, and we learned of it, from Robert Payne's *The Isles Of Greece*, only after we got home. Payne says it is a very small museum, only two rooms, and seldom visited. Its pride is simply the largest collection of Cycladic figures in the world. There are more than fifty of them, says Payne, "rarely more than three inches high, all carved out of marble and most of them representing a woman in the attitude of perfect repose, arms folded across her breast, face tilted back, no eyes, no mouth,* sharp triangular nose." Of course, if you miss Naxos, you will still see some astounding Cycladic work in Athens.

Naxos was Theseus' first port of call when, with beautiful Ariadne, he fled from Crete. He left her there, for reasons that are in dispute, though he himself felt no need of reasons for loving them and leaving them. For her part, she did not pine, for his place was immediately taken by Dionysios, and a god is presumably a better lover, and perhaps a better provider, than a mere hero.

Dionysios has always been big on Naxos; one of the most interesting of ancient remains concerns him. At a village called Apollona in the northeast corner of the island—some 45 hair-raising kilometers of nonroad from Naxia—is a still-active marble quarry. From it, stone was cut for the Kennedy memorial in Washington. From it, or from another of the Naxian quarries, came the great Apollo at Delos and, of course, the Naxian lions.

There remains in this hillside quarry a colossal unfinished statue of Dionysios. It would have been roughly 34 feet tall and, as the Delian Apollo announces on its base, "cut from one stone, statue and socle." It is, indeed, identified in most books as an

---

* Our note: Eyes and mouth and hair and clothing were painted on when the carvings were originally made, about 3000 B.C.; it's probably a blessing they're almost entirely worn off.

Apollo, and very likely gave the name to the village below it. We preen ourselves on having noticed that the figure is draped and thus certainly not Apollo. Professor MacKendrick, to whom we put the question, points out that the figure is not only draped (which would have made Apollo's sister Artemis a possibility), but bearded (which narrows the choice down to Dionysios, the lascivious Greek god who kept his clothes on).

The beard was actually the statue's undoing, for the stone split, and the lower half of the face slipped. In other times and places the head would have been cut off and a new one attached, but the Naxians evidently put special store by monolithic statues; so Dionysios was abandoned, even though he was rough-hewn and completely freed from the living rock. You can walk completely around and over him as he lies in the marble womb; not impossibly, he is more impressive in his unfinished and abandoned state than he would have been as one of a forest of similar monoliths.

There is at least one other monolith on Naxos, this one more than half finished, an undraped male, very likely an Apollo. It is sometimes confused with our Dionysios, though it is very much smaller (about 23 feet tall), has broken legs instead of a slipped beard, and lies in a field only a dozen kilometers from Naxia.

Naxos' other claim to fame is, of course, the Temple of Apollo on the tiny island of Palati in Naxia

Harbor. It is very old as Greek temples go, dating from the sixth century. The majestic marble doorway, some 20 feet high, is all that stands today; the effect of this glistening white rectangle against the blue sky is very grand.

TINOS (ΤΗΝΟΣ)

We once had a stopover of 45 minutes at Tinos, long enough to walk up the village street to the church of the Panagia Evangelistria. This is the great pilgrimage church of the Greek Orthodox world, and it attracts many visitors, especially on the feast day of August 15, but all through the year as well. The exterior is beautiful, with its gray and white marble courtyard and porticos of arches marching in rhythm, although the knowledge that some of the stones were taken from the Temple of Apollo on Delos casts a blight on one's pleasure. The interior seemed more curious than beautiful to our eyes. It is crammed with gold and silver votive offerings hanging from the chandeliers, many in the shape of an arm or a leg dedicated by someone hoping for or acknowledging a miraculous cure. There is a silver tree with golden oranges, and a miraculous icon which the faithful line up to kiss, after paying their drachmas. Some of the votive candles are 5 feet high. It is a scene of light, movement, and credulousness which we have not seen in any other Byzantine church.

16

RHODES

ΡΟΔΟΣ

A strong toun Rodez hit is,
The Castell is strong and fair I wis.
MATTHEW PARIS, *Purchas His Pilgrimes*

Rhodes has everything. It is a resort with a fine climate, luxurious vegetation, and good hotels. It has the great mediaeval walled city of the Knights of St. John, a picturesque Turkish quarter, and best of all, at Lindos, it has Classical ruins in a beautiful natural setting.

The ancient city of Rhodes dates from 408 B.C., when the three Dorian cities of the island, Ialysos, Kamiros, and Lindos, decided to found a new city as their capital, an interesting example of cooperation among city-states which has not, to our knowledge, been much commented on. The three original cities, all mentioned in the *Iliad,* have interesting ruins. The gridiron plan of Rhodes was laid out by Hippodamos of Miletos, one of the earliest town planners. The city flourished, and in Hellenistic times covered far more ground than did the mediaeval city. In 304 B.C. it successfully repulsed a year-long siege by Demetrios of Macedon, who was sarcastically dubbed *Poliorketes* ("Sacker of Cities").

His abandoned siege machine was used by the sculptor Chares of Lindos in building the famous Colossus of Rhodes, a bronze statue of Helios, the sun god, over 100 feet high, which is thought to have stood on the present site of Fort St. Nicholas. It definitely did not straddle the harbor, as we used to learn in school. Felled by an earthquake in 227 B.C., it was finally dismantled and sold for scrap metal in A.D. 653. Nine hundred camels carried it away, so the story goes.

Rhodes produced many other famous sculptors and statues. The Laocoön and the Winged Victory of Samothrace are attributed to Rhodian sculptors. The city still had over two thousand statues when Pliny saw it in the first century A.D. Rhodes was also famous for its school of rhetoric. Cicero, Caesar, Brutus, Cassius, and Lucretius all studied the art of oratory under Greek masters on Rhodes.

Excavations at all the ancient cities of the island have unearthed beautiful vases (decorated with naturalistic designs of animals and flowers) dating as far back as the tenth century B.C., but especially of the seventh and the sixth centuries.

Today another sort of Rhodian ware is much ap-

preciated. It is mostly in the form of brightly decorated plates in vivid blues and greens and shows a
Persian or Turkish influence. The finest pieces were
made in the sixteenth and seventeenth centuries and
are now in museums. But Rhodian ware is still being
made and sold in quantity. Some of the plates are
lovely. Some are garish. Smaller pieces—cups, tiny
whales, and the like—make excellent gifts or souvenirs.

Mediaeval Rhodes is unique. Nowhere else in
Greece, and at very few places in Western Europe,
can one see a similar complex of fourteenth- and
fifteenth-century ramparts and buildings so well preserved, or rather, like Carcassonne, so well restored.
In 1309 the Knights Hospitallers of St. John of Jerusalem (to give them their full name), a religious order
turned military in defense of the Holy Land, retreated
to Rhodes, which they captured after a campaign of
two years. They built the ramparts, the Hospital, the
hostels along the Street of the Knights, and the Palace
of the Grand Master, all there for us to see today, as
restored by the Italians, who in their turn took Rhodes
by force from the Turks in 1912, during the Balkan
Wars. At first the Greek population looked upon the
Italians as liberators, for they had suffered much
from the Turks, but when it became apparent that
the Italians had come to stay, the occupation was
resisted. Not until 1948, however, was Rhodes finally
returned to Greece, having been under foreign domi-

nation—Genoese, Frankish, Turkish, and Italian—for seven hundred long years.

It is a curious reflection on the ups and downs of history that when Delos was made a free port back in 166 B.C., Rhodes was ruined; when Rhodes was returned to Greece in 1948, in order to soften its absorption into the Greek economy, it was made a free port in its turn.

Rhodes and the other islands of the Dodekanese were still Italian when, in 1922, Greece invaded Turkey in a vain attempt to reclaim territories in Asia Minor inhabited by Greeks since the foundation of the Ionian cities three millennia ago. Consequently the Turks on Rhodes were not involved when Greece and Turkey had a compulsory exchange of population following this bitter war. The Greeks had the moral support of the Allies; the map of Europe and the Near East was being completely redrawn in the name of nationalism and the self-determination of peoples; Turkey had but lately been "the sick man of Europe." In spite of all this, the Greeks were defeated by Kemal Ataturk's revolutionary army, and a massive exchange of population was the negotiated result. At the time, the influx of refugees created great hardship, especially in Athens, but at least there was for a while no irridentism to perpetuate Greco-Turkish enmity, and the two countries, today both members of NATO, seemed to get along on the official level. The recent bloody "troubles" in Cyprus give an idea of what might have happened on a much larger scale if this Draconian solution had not been forced.

As a result of the above, Rhodes is almost the only place in Greece where you can see a Turkish quarter with mosques, minarets, and latticed windows, still inhabited by Turks—well worth a stroll after you have seen the town of the Knights.

The Knights built in a style that harks back to the Norman, with round arches, heavy pillars, and plain walls with few windows, reflecting both the military purpose of the architecture and the time lag in styles that is often found in the provinces. But the whole effect is lightened and refined by the warm tone of the stone, the crenelations at the top, the projecting corbels and gargoyles, the lovely decorative carving on capital and around windows, and the sculpted placques bearing the coats-of-arms of the various Grand Masters of the Order. Wonderful names they had—Foulques de Villaret, Pierre d'Aubusson, Villiers de l'Isle-Adam, Aimery d'Amboise. To anyone who loves the French language, these names are a delight.

Many a brave deed they did, as they fought the paynim foe in the name of our Lord, but many a sordid one, too. Pierre d'Aubusson earned a cardinal's hat by double-crossing the Sultan's son to whom he had offered protection, and he spent his last years extirpating the Jews from Rhodes. The Crusades may appear from a distance as a glittering spectacle and a great resurgence of the might of the West, but underneath the trappings of chivalry lies the horror of religious war and religious intolerance, when the Church of the Prince of Peace not only failed to promote peace on earth but incited violence.

Thackeray, who saw Rhodes in 1844, says in his "Notes of a Journey from Cornhill to Cairo":

The chivalrous relics at Rhodes are very superb. I know of no buildings whose stately and picturesque aspect seems to correspond better with one's notions of their proud founders. The towers and gates are war-like and strong, but beautiful and aristocratic; you see that they must have been high-bred gentlemen who built them. The edifices appear in almost as perfect a condition as when they were in the occupation of the noble knights of St. John; and they have this advantage over modern fortifications, that they are a thousand times more picturesque. Ancient war condescended to ornament itself, and built fine carved castles and vaulted gates: whereas, to judge from Gibraltar and Malta, nothing can be less romantic than the modern military architecture; which sternly regards the fighting, without in the least heeding the war-paint. . . . The Turks, who battered down chivalry, seem to be waiting their turn of destruction now. In the street of the Knights you see noble houses, surmounted by the noble escutcheons of superb knights, who lived there, and prayed, and quarrelled, and murdered the Turks; and were the most gallant pirates of the inland seas; and made vows of chastity, and robbed and ravished; and, professing humility, would admit none but nobility into their order; and died recommending themselves to sweet St. John, and calmly hoping for heaven in consideration of all the heathen they had slain. When this superb community was obliged to yield to courage as great as theirs, faith as sincere, and to robbers even more dexterous and audacious than the noblest knight who ever sang a canticle to the Virgin, these halls were filled by magnificent Pashas and Agas, who lived here in the intervals of wars, and having conquered its best champions, despised Christendom and chivalry pretty much as an Englishman despises a Frenchman . . . In the Crusades my wicked sympathies have always been with the Turks. They seem to me the best Christians of the two; more human, less brutally presumptuous about their own merits, and more generous in esteeming their neighbors. As far as I can get at the story, Saladin is a pearl of refinement compared to the brutal beef-eating Richard about whom Sir Walter Scott has led all the world astray.

As in many past eras when men's ideas seem strange and tarnished with inhumanity, their art and architecture still speak to us, and as tourists it is easier to turn our attention in that direction. Of all the buildings the Knights left, the loveliest is the hospital, a rival in beauty with the Hôtel-Dieu of Beaune, though very different: masculine where Beaune is feminine. It has an ogival entrance arch and galleried courtyard with loggia above reached by a grand stern staircase. It now houses the Archaeological Museum of Rhodes, with an impressive row of 6-foot burial vases in the geometric style, and some lovely sculptures, including an Aphrodite rising from the sea (the "Marine Venus" of Lawrence Durrell's book), and the grave stele of Krito and Timarista.

Adjacent to the hospital is the Street of the Knights, where each of the "Languages" or "Tongues"—France, Italy, Aragon, Castile, Provence, Germany—constructed an inn to receive its own chevaliers. These buildings are still used as dwellings, and their gardens are full of bougainvillaea and oleander.

The Palace of the Grand Masters withstood many a siege in its time, and was not greatly damaged when the Turks finally took the town in 1522 and the few remaining Knights retreated to Malta. But it was ruined by an explosion in 1856 and completely rebuilt to the original plans by the Italians. It suffers from a certain coldness, as restorations do, but it is a grand and imposing building. It does contain some ugly pieces of furniture, but it also has some beautiful ancient mosaics which the Italians removed from the island of Kos and installed on the floors of the palace. To the Greeks this was vandalism, since the palace was the headquarters of the Fascist governor, and the mosaics in the reception rooms were much walked on. Today tourists may look at them but are asked not to walk on them, and there is even talk of returning them to Kos.

A guided tour of the ramparts, on foot, leaves the courtyard of the palace every day at 9:00 A.M., and also at 3:00 P.M. every day in summer. Just a block or two to the south of the palace, still within the walls, lies the Turkish town. On to the mosques, or to the

Sound and Light spectacle performed nightly in the courtyard of the palace, when the Turkish siege of 1522 is recreated.

LINDOS (ΛΙΝΔΟΣ)

This also said Phocylides:
A tiny rock-built citadel
Is finer far, if ordered well,
Than all your frantic Ninevehs.
PHOCYLIDES
(Translation by C. M. Bowra)

Do not let traveler's fatigue or the desire for a swim keep you from Lindos. You can have your swim there; the beach of fine white sand is better than that at Rhodes itself. And if you want to get away from it all in the world's most heavenly spot, try Lindos. Our daughter and two college friends spent a week there; they chose well. There is no hotel in the little town (nor any running water), but they lodged with a lady named Marietta, whose donkey Lucile rode two years later. If she fussed over them as she fussed over us, it must have been fun. There are a few summer visitors, some artists perhaps, but no crowds. Many of the square white houses are decorated with carvings from the time of the Knights, and their courtyards have pebble mosaics in black and white. The pebble mosaic at the United Nations building is modeled on these floors and made from pebbles brought from Rhodian beaches. Above the town looms the acropolis with its temple, the goal of our excursion.

Guided tours run out from Rhodes, but there is no need for a guide. The local bus will do, if its schedule fits yours. Better spend a whole day at Lindos, or longer, much longer say we wistfully.

The 35-mile ride from Rhodes is through country beautiful with orange and pomegranate groves. In May oleanders blossom in the dry streambeds, making winding lines of pink between the bare hills.

Donkeys are available at the town square for the climb to the acropolis. It is not a hard climb, but a donkey ride is fun to try, at least once. Even a formidable German lady of our party, whose man-tailored suit and walking stick made her seem like a holdover from Bismarck's day, laughed and chatted, on donkeyback, like any schoolgirl.

The great rock of the acropolis rises sheer above the village, a true acropolis like that of Athens. You enter the sanctuary through the ruins of a Crusaders' fort and church, and climb a monumental staircase to a terrace supported by transverse barrel vaults. We think of the arch as the distinguishing feature of Roman building, but here at Lindos and at the Asklepeion on Kos, the Greeks were making real, though small, arches before 200 B.C..

The terrace above the vaults was enclosed on three sides by a stoa, a double colonnade roofed over against the sun, where the ancient Lindians met for business and talk. The Danish excavators and Italian restorers have re-erected enough of the yellow limestone columns to make a handsome sight against the skyline.

Up some more broad steps, through a propylaea (now gone), and back near the cliff's edge stands the temple of Athena Lindia, not large but lovely, built in the same golden stone in a simple Doric style. The fluting of the columns and the rhythmic alternation of metopes and triglyphs are the only decorations. Everything depends on harmony of line and proportion. The beauty of the setting and the relative simplicity of the buildings make the acropolis of Lindos very satisfying to the eye and to the mind.

To the left of the stoa there is a veritable field of statue bases, each inscribed with the name of the sculptor, a real find for scholars. Another find was the Lindian Chronicle, a marble discovered facedown on the floor of the Crusaders' church, inscribed with a list of gifts dedicated to Athena by mythical and historical personages. According to the list, many of the offerings were trophies taken in the Trojan War— Menelaos gave the helmet he had wrenched from Paris' head in the duel recounted in the third book of the *Iliad;* Kanopos, Menelaos' helmsman, gave his steering oars; Helen, two bracelets. When the tablet was put into the temple in 99 B.C., the gifts themselves had long since vanished (an early temple had burned in the fourth century), and the priests were careful to document their lists with references to earlier publications which named the donors and described the offerings. John Forsdyke, in his *Greece Before Homer,* says that "the prehistoric documents were authenticated by fraudulent inscriptions." He calls the tablet a "catalogue of antiquarian forgeries." Strong words. Did not Minos, King of Crete, really give a silver goblet? Nor Herakles two shields? But this is not the first nor the last instance of the chicanery of priests in promoting the cult of relics.

As we were descending from the acropolis and admiring a 15-foot trireme carved in high relief in the rock, a French light cruiser came steaming by. All hands had been mustered on deck, and over the loudspeaker came an erudite lecture on ancient Lindos in lucid French.

For those who have time at Lindos and can resist the lure of the beach, there is a little Byzantine church whose late (eighteenth-century) frescoes are admired, an ancient theater on the west side of the acropolis, and a few minutes walk from town, the so-called tomb of Cleobulus, tyrant of Lindos in the sixth century, and one of the Seven Sages of the ancient world. The poet Simonides ridiculed Cleobulus' belief in the imperishability of monuments:

> *Thoughtful men their praise withhold*
> *From Lindian Cleobulus. He defied*
> *Running rivers, spring flowers, burning gold*
> *Of sun and moon, and swirling ocean pools*

In strength to outbide
A stone.
The gods are strong alone.
Marble our hands can break to bits.
Those Lindian wits
Are but a fool's.

(Translation by T. F. Higham)

Much marble has indeed been broken to bits. But much remains, the gods be praised.

17

CRETE

ΚΡΗΤΗ

The labyrinth was constructed by Daedalus, for he was an excellent architect and the first inventor of images.
APOLLODOROS, *The Library*
(Translation by J. G. Frazer)

From Rhodes a short hop by air takes you to Herakleion, and back to the Bronze Age of the second millennium B.C., when Europe's first civilization flowered brilliantly on the island of Crete. Favored by nature with a mild climate, and protected by their command of the sea from fear of invasion, the Minoans devoted their energies to the refinements of living. Theirs was a very human civilization in comparison with those of Assyria and Egypt—they built no grandiose monuments, but pleasure palaces. This civilization lasted for almost a thousand years before it was suddenly extinguished by earthquake, invasion, or both. One disputed theory holds that the coastal towns and palaces were destroyed by tidal waves and earthquakes in conjunction with the great volcanic explosion circa 1520 B.C. which threw most of the

island of Thera (modern Santorini) into the sea; that
the palace of Knossos lasted until 1400 B.C., by which
time the Mycenaeans were masters on Crete, which
continued to be a rich land (in the *Iliad*'s catalogue of
ships Crete sent eighty ships to the Trojan War as
against nine from Rhodes); and that both Mycenae
and Crete were overrun by the Dorians about 1100
B.C.; then followed the Dark Ages.

Since those days three thousand years ago Crete
has never been a center of power (although memories
of past glories persisted in the legends of King Minos,
Daedalos, the labyrinth, and the Minotaur), but has
had a long history of oppression and resistance to
oppressors, including a siege lasting twenty-four years
before the Venetians surrendered to the Turks in
1669. Throughout the nineteenth century, after the
rest of Greece was free, the many uprisings by Cretan
patriots were savagely repressed by the Turks, and
"savagely repressed" is not an idle phrase. Just one
example among many: In 1824 the Turks set fire to
piles of brushwood at the mouth of the cave of
Melidoni where several hundred Cretans, including
women and children, had taken refuge from bands of
Turkish marauders. All were suffocated. It couldn't
have been done better with flame throwers.

In 1898 (only yesterday) the Cretans won their
autonomy. In our lifetime Cretan valor reached a
climax in the heroic attempt by Cretans and British
Commonwealth troops to stem the German parachute

invasion of May, 1941. Although organized resistance lasted only ten days, it took so many lives and planes that the German High Command considered the operation a failure. But Crete was once again an occupied country, and for three and a half years Cretans continued the struggle as guerrillas, and their villages suffered reprisals.

As a result of this bloody history, there is an intensity, even a ferocity about the Cretan character, not, fortunately, directed toward the tourist, who meets only friendliness and hospitality. But one observes that old traditions endure. Even today in downtown Herakleion you will see men in baggy trousers, with fierce upturned mustachios, and daggers in their belts. Read Nikos Kazantzakis's novel *Freedom and Death* to learn what formed these men.

Crete has great mountain ranges, where shepherds guard their sheep in summer pastures near the caves which sheltered Zeus from angry Kronos. At least two caves claim the honor, one on Mount Dikte and one on Mount Ida. If you are strong and agile, you may climb to see these caves. But the twin lodestones that draw us all to Crete are the Palace of Knossos, the great center of Minoan civilization, which lies just outside of Herakleion, and the Archaeological Museum of Herakleion, whose rooms hold marvels that make it one of the world's great museums.

Crete requires some homework, as it should, if you are to encompass a whole civilization in a few days.

An amateur archaeologist appropriately named Minos Kalokairinos discovered the site of Knossos and un- covered some storerooms in 1878, and Heinrich Schliemann arrived full of hopes in 1889, but their efforts were obstructed by the Turks, and it fell to Sir Arthur Evans, after independence came, to buy the site and in 1898 start the excavation and the re- construction of the Palace of Knossos which, for the rest of his life, absorbed his interest and his money (he spent £250,000 from his own pocket). His sister, Joan Evans, has written that he had come to the site "in hope of finding a seal impression and a clay tab- let, and Time and Chance had led him to discover a civilization."

Although some details are contested in the elab- orate time scheme that Evans drew up, and some scholars deplore the amount of reconstructing he did (with a view to preserving the ruins as well as dis- playing them), there is general agreement that his work was splendid in scope and in result. Certainly every tourist should pay his respects to Evans's genius. The palace complex he uncovered contained 1,300 rooms on several levels, and if it were not for Evans's work in re-erecting some of the walls, pillars, and stairways, it would be just a hodgepodge to the un- initiate. As it is, we are able to gain a vivid picture of the beauty and luxury in which these people lived.

The Minoan palace was an entirely different thing from the Classical temple. One room was added to

another in a seemingly haphazard design. The resulting maze may be, in fact, the only foundation for the
legend of the fearsome labyrinth. But the Minoan
builders had more skill than one might think from a
glance at the site plan. Courtyards, lightwells, and
breezeways provided sun and air, and every guide
shows every tourist the famous plumbing system,
with three separate water lines—one for drinking,
one for washing, and one for carrying off the waste.
Like all of us, the guides take a very natural pride
in the accomplishments of their ancestors, however
remote.

Because of the complexity of the palace plan, we
strongly recommend that you do not try to stumble
about Knossos with your nose in a guidebook, but that
you hire a guide, either through your travel agent,
through the Greek National Tourist Office on 25th
August Street, Herakleion, or by inquiring at the museum. We had the good fortune to be guided by Mr.
Karousos, a very learned gentleman who spoke excellent English, the best guide we had in Greece. It
would be ideal to have Mr. Karousos show you around
Knossos without thirty or forty other people in your
party. Do try to get him; it would be worth your while
to write ahead to the museum and reserve his services
for a morning or a day.

The Palace of Knossos stands on a knoll in a lovely
cup-shaped valley surrounded by hills which were
wooded in Pliny's time. At its foot runs the little

river Kairatos which connected it with the port called
Amnisos, and in ancient times was navigable by small
boats, though now it is dry except in winter. Amnisos
has acquired new fame lately; the first word deci-
phered by the architect and amateur archaeologist Michael Ventris when he broke Linear B was *Amnisos*.
But in spite of the fact that we can now read their
language, the palace ruins, the artifacts found in
them, in the tombs, and in the cave sanctuaries, are
still the source of most of our information about the
Minoans, and even these are subject to various inter-
pretations.

Here we might say a word about the frustration
which sometimes overtakes the tourist in viewing pre-
Homeric sites. One is told categorically that this part
of the ruins was of such and such a period, this part
earlier or later, that here was the Sacred Gate, here
the priests' rooms, here the Queen's chamber, that
here was a frieze with a procession of 350 men. How
do they know? One looks around and there is so little
left to see. George Mylonas, a Greek who excavated at
Mycenae, has said that the reward of archaeology is
"to infer from withered flowers the hour of their
bloom." But how?

In the first place, archaeologists know much more
than we do. Everything they see says much more to
them. *The Mute Stones Speak, The Greek Stones
Speak* states MacKendrick in the titles of his books.
Sometimes written records or inscriptions which are

incomprehensible to the layman help the scholar. A friend of ours who took a British Hellenic Cruise up the Nile tells that when the group was being shown some wall paintings depicting scenes from the life of an Egyptian princess, she asked the distinguished professor who was leading them how it was known that this was a princess, not a goddess. "Why," he said, impatient at such a *foolish* question, "why, it says so right there," and he pointed to some hieroglyphics.

It should be remembered also that the site as the archaeologists uncover it looks quite different from what we see as tourists years later. As each layer is uncovered, down to the deepest and oldest, the finds are correlated with what has been found elsewhere, especially in Egypt, where written inscriptions have helped to establish a relatively firm set of dates, although these are now being questioned. Pottery is especially useful. As Herbert J. Muller says, "Potsherds are really immortal: bones, wood, and metal may return to dust, but baked clay never does." Some experts know to the last sherd every bit of pottery found in the Mediterranean and the Near East. But the pottery and the jewelry and the statuary are usually carried away to the museum, leaving the tourist with many fewer clues than the excavators had. The greatest loss, though a necessary one, is the frescoes, which often crumble when exposed to the air. One feels this at Mycenae and Tiryns much more than at Knossos, because Evans had with him some accomplished artists, Piet de Jong and the Gillièrons, father and son, who copied the frescoes before they disintegrated. The original fragments, pieced together, are in the museum. Many copies have been put up at the site, adding enormously to the beauty and drama of Knossos.

With the possible exception of the Chinese, there have been no artists in all the centuries to surpass the Minoans in the naturalistic rendering of flowers and animals. The lily, the lotus, the crocus that bloom on the walls of Knossos; the pheasant, the crouching cat, the blue monkey, the leaping dolphins, and the sinuous octopi have never been painted with more life and beauty. Minoan artists infused the same life into their human figures. The bull leapers, the "Prince of the Lilies," and especially the famous young lady called "the Parisienne," with her great dark eye, saucy profile, and proud bosom, are all charged with life and movement. Neither reproductions in books nor the copies at the site, welcome as they are, can give a true idea of this tremendous artistic achievement. You must go to the museum, to the second floor, and sit and look at these people in the frescoes, so graceful, so elegant, so sophisticated—in a word, so modern.

The museum has other evidence of unsurpassed Minoan craftmanship; notably the lovely Kamares ware, with its strong decoration in yellow, red, and white on a black ground; sometimes the pottery itself is so incredibly thin it is called "eggshell ware." Look at the gold jewelry, the utterly simple daisy sprays and leaves from Mochlos and the gorgeous pendant from Mallia in the shape of two queen bees who clasp a honeycomb made of tiny beads of gold so fine that modern goldsmiths cannot do the like (such tiny beads melt under the soldering iron, or so we were told). See the Harvester Vase, with its rhythms of marching men with their flails over their shoulders, which makes one think of Uccello battle paintings. The little sealstones and carved gems in the cases provide a history of Minoan culture in miniature. They are so important that scholars pore over enlarged reproductions of them. Did those artists use the magnifying glass in their work? There is some evidence that they did, in the form of natural crystals. Notice the cult objects—the bulls' heads, the snake goddess, the double axes (labrys) of gold or bronze. This museum is so full of riches that it is a good idea, as in Athens, to make two trips to it, even if you are in Crete only for two days; Knossos and the museum one day, the museum and Phaestos or Mallia the next, and a return trip to Knossos if possible.

It is hard to choose between Phaestos and Mallia; but if you must select one or the other because of a tight schedule, do it along these lines. If you would like to see more of the interior of Crete and visit another great Minoan palace, hire a car or take the excursion bus to Phaestos. If you are aching for a relaxing swim on a sandy beach, go to Mallia, spend an hour exploring the palace ruins, and five minutes later you can take a dip in the ocean.

Mallia is about 34 kilometers east of Herakleion. A little beyond the Florida Beach you pass a road to the right which leads to the Cave of Eilithyia, sacred to the goddess of childbirth since Neolithic times, and mentioned in the *Odyssey*. You may enter the cave and see the sacred stalagmites, if that takes your fancy.

The ruins of the provincial palace of Mallia lie near the coast in the shadow of the Lasithi Mountains, which make a most dramatic backdrop to the peaceful plain where bananas grow and windmills turn. The most unusual feature of the ruins is a round stone called a kernos with thirty-four small circular depressions around the rim. It is thought that offerings of seeds were placed there to ensure the fertility of the crops.

A trip to Phaestos means a slightly longer expedition—a ride of a little over an hour each way.

The road passes first through vineyard and table-grape country, then over a formidable mountain pass and down into the fertile plain of Messara, large by Greek standards, where wheat is grown and still threshed on round stone threshing floors, although we did see a few threshing machines. Mount Ida towers over the plain to the west, the Lasithi Mountains are to the east, and a lower range of mountains hides the sea. Phaestos on its little hill looks to the mountains on every horizon.

The view is reason enough for making a trip to Phaestos, but there is also the palace, which was second in size and spendor to Knossos, and may even have surpassed it in the first palace period. It has been excavated, but not reconstructed. Its great staircase and courtyard, made of gypsum, a stone easily available on the flanks of Mount Ida, and soft enough to be cut easily with bronze tools, glisten dazzling white in the sun. This courtyard is only slightly smaller than the one at Knossos and is more impressively monumental. The most important single find at Phaestos is a round black disk, now in the museum at Herakleion, stamped in hieroglyphics. Professor Cyrus H. Gordon of Brandeis has announced the decipherment of the disk.

For the visit to Phaestos, we engaged one of the young lady graduates of the Guide School, who rode out with us from Herakleion. She did an adequate but uninspired job, perhaps because she was suffering from hay fever. We should have done better to rely, as some British friends did, on the local caretaker, who is delighted to show off his palace, and is apparently a friendly sort. When he learned that it was our British friend's birthday he insisted on stretching his 5'6" to the Britisher's 6'2", and giving him a big buss on each cheek. This is the same Alexandros, although older by twenty-four years, in whose company Henry Miller had such an emotional binge, moved by the tremendous beauty of Phaestos, and influenced perhaps by the *mavrodaphne* (dessert wine) Alexandros gave him at lunch. Miller calls Phaestos the abode of queens, "feminine through and through." Robert Payne calls it "naked power in all its majesty." You are entitled to form your own opinion.

Only 2 miles from Phaestos is another site of great interest, the Minoan villa of Agia Triada, which was perhaps a summer palace, for the sea came close in those days. It is famous for its frescoes, for a painted sarcophagus, and for the Harvester and the Chieftain Vases, all found here and now in the museum in Herakleion.

John Bowman's *Guide to Crete* says that it is an easy 45-minute walk from Phaestos. If you are tempted to walk, you should take into account that Bowman is an Englishman, and perhaps one of those mad ones who go out in the midday sun. In Greek legend, when a god wanted to addle a maiden's wits the better to seduce her, he lured her into the midday sun. Noon was the witching hour, rather than midnight, as with Northern peoples.

About 10 miles south of Phaestos on the coast which looks toward Africa is the harbor of Kaloi Limenes, the Fair Havens of Acts 27, where St. Paul's ship put in when he voyaged to Rome to be brought before Caesar. Kaloi Limencs is probably not worth a visit, but a nearer seaside town, Matala, can be recommended to the hardy or leisurely traveler, in spite of poor roads. At Matala, by a lovely cove with good bathing, a strange cliff of soft yellow stone, or hard yellow sand, rises sheer from the sea. It is honeycombed with man-made caves, still used as dwellings as they were in Neolithic times. You might want to stay overnight to take advantage of the swimming. The Tourist Pavilion at Phaestos has a few dormitory rooms if you are willing to rough it, and it is said that there will be one at Matala soon.

On the return trip to Herakleion you will want to stop briefly at Gortyn, which figures in legend as the place where Europa and Zeus celebrated their wedding, their progeny being the kings Minos and Rhadymanthos. But Gortyn was not prominent in Minoan times; the city reached its peak under the Romans, when it was the capital of the province of Crete and Cyrenaica. An Italian traveler of the fifteenth century wrote that he "counted two thousand columns and statues upturned by time. In grandeur it is the equal of our Florence." There are ruins from Classic and Hellenistic times hidden amid the olive trees on both sides of the highway, but the focus of interest at Gortyn is the famous Law Code, to be found to the left of the highway behind the sixth-century (A.D.) Basilica of Agios Titos, named for the same Titus whom St. Paul appointed as first Bishop of Crete. In his Epistle to Titus (1: 12–13) Paul said: "One of themselves, even a prophet of their own, said, The Cretians are always liars, evil beasts, slow bellies. This witness is true. Wherefore rebuke them sharply, that they may be sound in the faith."

The Law Code of Gortyn is thought to date from the middle fifth century B.C. It is an inscription of over 17,000 characters carved on yellow limestone blocks and deals with civil matters such as divorce, dowries, adoption, inheritance rights, the position of slaves. The Romans moved it from its original position in the Greek Agora and set it up behind their Odeon. When Italian archaeologists excavated the site in the 1880's, the blocks were found scattered in the mill stream; now they stand again behind the Odeon, and are protected by a roof. The code is inscribed in an archaic Dorian Greek which reads from left to right and back again, the so-called "ox-plough script." Some of its letters, such as "c," "v," and medial "s" are obsolete in modern Greek, indeed in Classical Greek. Its artistic and historic interest make a stop well worthwhile.

Before leaving Herakleion, if you are interested in the Byzantine, step into the cathedral to see the six icons painted by Michael Damaskinos, the sixteenth-century contemporary of El Greco (also a Cretan).

In his *First Pythian Ode*, Pindar addresses Apollo's lyre of gold in lines of magical evocativeness:

The light foot hears you, and the brightness begins:
Your notes compel the singer
When to lead out the dance.
(Translation by H. T. Wade-Gery and C. M. Bowra)

The light foot, at any rate, still is seen in Greece; and one of the best places to see it is at the Glass House Restaurant near the Herakleion waterfront, which has a team of three dancers in Cretan costume who satisfied some of our desire to see Greek folk dancing. The men, tall and lithe, were especially good dancers, and the girl, with her lovely slim body and delicate profile, was a joy to look upon, which is as it should be in Greek dancing, where women are passive, a reflection of the old idea that women's place was in the home and out of sight, except when serving the heroic men.

Cretan dances are very old. It has even been suggested that the spectacular leaps of the male dancers have their origins in the sacred bull dances at the court of King Minos.

In describing the shield that Hephaestos made for Achilles, Homer says:

He made a dancing place like that which Daedalus made of old for fair Ariadne. There young men were dancing and girls you would give many cattle for, with their arms on one another's forearms. The girls were in fair linen, the young men in shirts, well made and lightly oiled. The girls were crowned with leaves and the young men had knives of gold hanging from silver cords. Sometimes they would dance in a ring, as a potter will sit with his wheel between his hands seeing if it will run;

sometimes they would step in lines to meet each other. And a great company stood round in joy, while two tumblers whirled in the middle giving the measure.

Iliad, Book XVIII
(Translation by I. A. Richards)

Scenes not too different from this may be seen today.

Greek music is strange to our ears, especially the wailing voices of the songs; but it has rhythm to wake the dead and make them dance. One of the musicians accompanying the dancers at the Glass House played the *lyra,* not a lyre but an ancient instrument shaped like a small lute that is held on the knee and bowed ceaselessly at lightning speed. The clarinet is prominent in these small orchestras, taking the place of the *aulos,* the double reed pipe played by the Greeks since sometime in the third millennium B.C. Did you notice the marble statuettes of the lyre player and the aulos player in the Cycladic room of the National Museum in Athens? They are so cool in their free-flowing lines that they might have come from a sculptor's workshop of the twentieth century A.D. instead of the twentieth century B.C. The Metropolitan Museum of Art in New York has some fine examples of Cycladic work.

Delphi and Delos both claimed to be the center of the world. Crete made no such claim; yet it had a better right to the title. Cyrus Gordon tells us that the Minoans were Northwest Semites (that is, in

Greek terms, Phoenicians) who had migrated to the Nile Delta before moving on to their mid-Mediterranean home. They built a brilliant civilization that stretched from Asia, over all the islands, to mainland Greece, and beyond. The King James Version refers to the inhabitants of the seacoast as Cherethites (Zeph. 2:5), but in the original the name is Kretim. The 1400 B.C. tablets from Ugarit on the Syrian coast include the *Epic of Kret*. The Phoenician Cadmus founded Thebes; his sister Europa was mother of Minos . . . From Crete the imagination races outward. We have seen so much of the ancient world. Who can doubt that we must see more?

APPENDIX I

THE GREEK LANGUAGE

One of the great achievements of the ancient Greeks was to develop a reformed alphabet and put it at the disposal of free citizens not subject to a priestly hierarchy . . . Secular curiosity flourished in the ancient world only where Greek was the language of daily use.

LANCELOT HOGBEN, *The Mother Tongue*

What can we usefully say about the Greek language? Only that you can get along splendidly in Greece without knowing a word of Greek, but that it is fun to learn a little; and that Greek is much easier than it looks, once you penetrate the camouflage of that unfamiliar alphabet. The alphabet is the first thing to learn. Do five letters a day, upper and lower case, please; they are quite different. Menus are usually in lower case, and sometimes handwritten, in which event you throw yourself on the mercy of the waiter, who probably speaks a little English anyhow. If you are in the country, you simply walk into the kitchen and point; that is the custom, so you need not feel embarrassed. Once you know the alphabet many words will be familiar even though they do not seem so at first. Σούπα (*soúpa*) is obviously soup; φρούτα (*fróuta*), fruit; πατάτες (*patátes*), potatoes; σαλάτα (*saláta*), salad; λεμόνι (*lemóni*), lemon; καφές (*kafés*), coffee; etc.; It is not too hard to remember that ζάχαρη (*záchari*) is sugar.

243

Road signs (but not street signs) are printed in both Greek and Roman letters. In Athens it helps to know that an "ou" or "ous" ending is a sign of the genitive case. ΟΔΟΣ ΕΡΜΟΥ (Odos Ermou) is the Street of Hermes; ΠΕΡΙΚΛΕΟΥΣ (Perikleous) is Pericles' Street; ΑΔΡΙΑΝΟΥ (Adrianou), the Street of Hadrian.

One of the by-products of learning the Greek alphabet is the insight it gives you into the way in which scholars decipher unknown languages. For example, on our first day in Athens we saw a billboard with the inscription: ΕΡΑΚΛΕΣ whose meaning we quickly unlocked by sounding out the letters: (H)erakles. How simple and obvious.

The principle, however, is that used by Ventris and the rest: writing stands for *sounds*. Not uncommonly a given symbol will be used for the same sound in several languages, though of course one can be fooled (the Greek P = our R, etc.) Also the patterns of sounds—relative frequency, use at ends of words, etc.—have been worked out for all known languages. With such clues and a great deal of painstaking work Linear B was broken and Linear A is being broken.

When a break begins, feedback occurs. The billboard we saw in Athens carried a picture of a bag and a mason's trowel. In America there is at least one Hercules Cement Company; so we were emboldened to take a stab at the second word on the billboard: ΤΣΙΜΕΝΤΟ.

Transliterated, this is Tsimento, which looks like nothing in particular; but sounded out it is obviously related to *cement,* which confirms us in our interpretation of the picture and our translation of the name.*

Unless you are a natural linguist of marked ability you will need many hours of study to benefit much from the

---

* For a full and fascinating discussion of all this, see John Chadwick: *The Decipherment of Linear B.*

phrase books or the records, though every little bit helps. We do not advise investing in a set of records. One disk will provide all the Greek you can absorb. Take a phrase book with you. *Say It in Modern Greek* in the Dover series is a good one. In a pinch you can point to the sentences you cannot quite say.

Perhaps you will become expert enough to decipher the names of the gods carved on the priests' chairs at the Theater of Dionysios, or an inscription or two at Eleusis. A simple pleasure, but oddly exhilarating. At the very least you can learn a few greetings and the words for "please" and "thank you." If you sometimes come across the greeting *yia sou* and sometimes *yia sas* ("your health"), it is merely because the former is in the singular and the latter in the plural. Another common greeting is χαίρετε (*haírete*), with that bothersome χ, transliterated by "ch" or simply "h," but pronounced midway between the two, like the "ch" in the Scottish *loch*, the German *ich*, or the Hebrew *Hanukkah*.

The rules of pronunciation are tricky at first, not because of any irregularity in Greek, but because for us English-speakers certain letters are pronounced differently from what we expect. The vowels η, ι, and υ when between two consonants, and the diphthongs οι, ει, and υι are all pronounced like the "i" in "machine." β (lower case: ϐ) is not pronounced "b" but "v"; Δ(δ) is not "d" but the dull "th" of our "these" and "those." The phrase books list all these little nuances, but without practice they are hard to remember in the stress of conversation. One curiosity is the Greek way of writing our sound "b." It appears as μπ, so that μπάρ (*bár*) is bar, and μπίρα (*bíra*) is beer (pronounced BEER-a). The many signs saying FIX are merely advertising a beer named after a German brewer, Fuchs. If you need gas, look for the MOMΠIΛ (Mobil) signs.

Pay attention to the accent marks in your phrase book. The accented syllable is always stressed. This gives you a real advantage over the poor souls learning English, who have to cope with a stress which wanders from syllable to syllable, they know not where or why.

On the other hand, disregard the breathing marks (inverted commas) which appear over or before certain initial vowels. They have no function now, though in ancient Greek they indicated that the vowel should be aspirated. This is why many Greek words beginning with a vowel have been transliterated into English with an initial "H" added. Ἑλλας becomes Hellas, οἱ πολλοί becomes hoi polloi (the "oi" is now pronounced like the "i" in "machine"; Greek no longer has the ugly "oy" sound that we give it in English). Learn to drop your aitches mentally.

A word about spelling: There is no generally recognized spelling of Greek proper names in English, nor is there any consistent set of principles for the purpose. We used to get our Greek through the Latin—the very name "Greece" is a mispronunciation of the Latin *Graecia;* the Greeks call their land *Hellas* and have done so for twenty-five hundred years, or as long as they've called it anything.

An unnecessary and irritating source of confusion comes down from the Romans, by way of the Etruscans: the use of "c" instead of "k" for the Greek *kappa.* Following the lead of many contemporary scholars, we have put back the "k" in Greek names where it does not alter the pronunciation. But sometimes a "c" is soft in English, as in Mycenae and Cyclades. In such cases the restoration of the "k" would cause too great a wrench. The other exception is on the grounds of familiarity: everyone is so accustomed to reading Acropolis and Corinth that we haven't presumed to make the change from "c" to "k."

The Romans also changed the "os" endings to "us." We have changed them back.

Yet we certainly haven't been consistent. A few examples of familiar names will show how impossible the goal is: Athens is, in part, an English *translation* (the "s" is there because the Greek AΘHNAI is a plural); Delphi, however, is a *Latin* rendering of the plural ΔΕΛΦΟΙ; Delos is a *transcription* of the sound of the Greek ΔHΛOΣ; Brauron is a *transliteration* of the Ancient Greek BPAYPΩN, though the Modern Greek sounds like Vravrona.

We're not altogether happy with what we've done, but we hope our readers won't be bothered by it. Indeed, one should not be bothered by any spelling of Greek names one runs into anywhere but should be prepared for imaginative jumps from one system to another. Greek maps identify a certain island as either ῪΔPA (capital letters) or Ὑδρα (lower case); in various books and on various maps in our collection the same place turns up as Hydra, Hydrea, Idhra, Idra, Ithra, Ydra, and Ythra. The first is most common and is the one we've settled on; the last probably comes closest to indicating the Modern Greek pronunciation.

Occasionally a guide will misguidedly use the Roman names for the gods and goddesses. One sometimes hears of Mars and Venus instead of Ares and Aphrodite. Let us not encourage this barbarism by falling in with it, but show that we know the proper Greek names, even though anglicized, for the Greek gods.

Here is a cautionary tale, albeit a mild one, which illustrates several of the points in this chapter. On our very first day with a car, as we left Athens for Daphne, we came to a traffic circle and followed a sign which said ΠΑΡΝΗΣ. After some miles we started climbing a very steep mountain road with great switchbacks. There was no turning back until we reached the top. There in a pine grove we met some workmen and said to them, "Daphne, Daphne." No sign of comprehension. Finally we thought to say "Thaphne," but not until we said "Thaphné," with the accent on the second syllable, did we make our destination clear and get directions to turn back. ΠΑΡΝΗΣ, the truth slowly dawned, is Parnes. Daphne would be ΔΑΦΝΗ. A silly mistake, which a little more homework with the Greek alphabet would have obviated, but luckily no harm done. Mount Parnes has wonderful views over Attica.

And so *yia sas,* and a good trip (καλὸ ταζίδι)!

APPENDIX 2

BOOKS

> *In spite of the valuable expositions of so many commentators, our stock of information respecting the ancient world remains lamentably inadequate to the demands of an enlightened curiosity.*
>
> GEORGE GROTE, *History of Greece*

It is fashionable to decry Baedeker-like guidebooks. They obviously do not make good consecutive reading, and they are not much help in planning a trip (else why are you reading this?). But if you want to *know* what you are looking at, instead of merely having a vague impression of it, you have two choices: use a guidebook, or hire a guide. The former is cheaper and generally more accurate. Sometimes, on a complicated site, you will want a guide; but you will always have use for a guidebook.

There are now three reasonably good English-language guidebooks to Greece: Nagel's, the Blue Guide, and Hachette's ($8 to $10 each). The original French edition of Hachette's is known as *le Guide Bleu,* but it is not to be confused with the Blue Guide; the similarity of titles was doubtless arranged by the Delphic Oracle. Of the three, Nagel's is the simplest, is generally accurate, and generally gives the lay traveler what he wants to know and not much more. The others are possibly more de-

tailed than necessary for ordinary use; yet they are valuable reference books and can be counted on to contain
all sorts of out-of-the-way information. We have relied
on Hachette's. The Fodor guide is not recommended.
None of the omnibus guides to all-Europe-at-once is of
any use.

No really satisfactory map of Greece has come to our
notice. The one issued by the National Tourist Office is
small in scale, out of date, and not without error. British
Petroleum (Shell) and Mobil both put out better ones,
but these, too, are out of date, since the Greeks, like
everyone else, are building roads apace. The maps in
Hachette's are fair enough; those in Nagel's are not so
good.

You should, nevertheless, write the Greek National
Tourist Organization, 601 Fifth Avenue, New York, for
their literature. Even though their map of the whole
country is inferior, their map of Athens is useful, and
some of their brochures are interesting if you make
proper allowance for the art of the public relations man.

As remarked in Chapter 2, *Greece on $5. a Day* (Pocket
Books, $1.95) is worth consulting if you plan to make
your own reservations.

BACKGROUND

An indispensable book is Paul MacKendrick's *The Greek
Stones Speak* (St. Martin's, $7.50; New American Library,
95¢), the story of archaeology in Greek lands. With
delightful wit and impeccable scholarship, it describes
the principal sites and tells something of how they were
discovered and what has been learned from them. One
of its useful features is that it is profusely (if sloppily)

illustrated. Read it before you go, and take it with you for reference.

If your knowledge of Greek history, arts, and letters is weak, a good book to start with is Robert Payne's *Ancient Greece* (Norton, $8.95). A more scholarly (and shorter) introduction is M. Rostovtzeff's *Greece* (Oxford, $2.25).

There are several good books on what is called the Greek spirit. The best (and shortest) is probably M. I. Finley's *The Ancient Greeks* (Viking Compass Books, $1.45), though H. D. F. Kitto's *The Greeks* (Penguin, $1.25) and C. M. Bowra's *The Greek Experience* (New American Library, 50¢) are not far behind it.

A famous and fascinating book is Edith Hamilton's *The Greek Way* (Norton Library, 95¢), which, with its sequel, *The Echo of Greece* (Norton Library, $1.25), uses Greek literature as a springboard to a discussion of the meaning of Greece.

Edith Hamilton, again, is the best introducer of the myths, in her *Mythology* (New American Library, 60¢), though the principal ones are set forth in Payne's *Ancient Greece*, mentioned above. For reference, you will want to take along with you H. J. Rose's *Handbook of Greek Mythology* (Dutton, $1.55). Robert Graves's *The Greek Myths* (Penguin, $2.90) has a lot of material not in the other books, but is crotchety and cryptic.

Greece has called into being many great and illuminating works of scholarship. For the most part these are put out of the layman's reach by the language barrier, if by nothing else. If, however, you really get caught by Greece, there are two you will want, sooner or later, to turn to: E. R. Dodds's *The Greeks and the Irrational* (University of California, $1.95) and Cedric H. Whitman's *Homer and the Heroic Tradition* (Norton Library, $1.95): not for beginners, but not to be missed either.

Other books, useful in their different ways, are John Chadwick's *The Decipherment of Linear B* (Modern Library, 95¢); Kathleen Freeman's *Greek City-States* (Norton Library, $1.65); and C. E. Robinson's *Everyday Life in Ancient Greece* (Oxford, $1.25).

PREHISTORY

The late prehistory, or protohistory, of Greece—that is, the story of what happened between 3000 and 700 B.C.— is one of the most rapidly changing of disciplines. What was well established ten years ago is contradicted today, and today's received doctrine is likely to suffer a similar fate tomorrow. The resulting confusion need not upset the traveler, for most of what will impress him in Greece dates from the fifth and fourth centuries; but he may find his imagination engaged and his curiosity piqued. It is a fascinating subject, and not the least of it is the feeling everyone has that great discoveries are around the corner.

The subject is of course touched on in several of the books mentioned under other headings. In addition, there are several that make it their primary subject and are within a layman's grasp. Among the most stimulating are three books by Professor Cyrus M. Gordon of Brandeis, who has announced the decipherment not only of Linear A but also the Phaestos Disk. We strongly recommend Professor Gordon's *The Ancient Near East* (Norton Library, $1.75), his *The Common Background of Greek and Hebrew Civilizations* (Norton Library, $1.65), and his *Ugarit and Minoan Crete* (Norton, $7.50).

Five other books on prehistory may be mentioned: John Forsdyke's *Greece Before Homer* (Norton Library, $1.55), an amusing analysis of problems of chronology;

R. W. Hutchinson's *Prehistoric Crete* (Penguin, $1.95), a detailed summary; J. D. S. Pendlebury's *The Archaeology of Crete* (Norton Library, $1.75), called by Hutchinson "easily the best general account of Minoan culture"; L. R. Palmer's *Mycenaeans and Minoans* (Knopf, $6.95); and C. G. Starr's *The Origins of Greek Civilization* (Knopf, $8.50).

LITERATURE

At this point you will probably want to dip into what the Greeks wrote themselves. A good sampling of poetry, some of it in translations of surpassing beauty, appears in *The Oxford Book of Greek Verse in Translation* (Oxford, $5.75). A smaller selection has been edited by Moses Hadas for the Modern Library ($2.45).

You will certainly want to read Aeschylus' *Agamemnon* before you go to Mycenae. Edith Hamilton has a beautiful translation in her *Three Greek Plays* (Norton Library, 95¢), and the entire Orestean trilogy has been translated by Richmond Lattimore (University of Chicago, $1.50) and Paul Roche (New American Library, 75¢).

Among the other classics you have been meaning to read sometime are Herodotos and Thucydides. Now is the time to do it.

And of course there is Homer. To those who do not know the original, the various translations of Richards, Rieu, Rouse, Fitzgerald, and Lattimore all sound good; the last two, both in verse, are currently the most highly regarded, but a new *Odyssey* by Albert Cook will make a strong bid for supremacy.

ART BOOKS

Since the end of the war, there has been an enormous output of books on art, including Greek art. Unfortunately many of them are thrown together for the Christmas gift market and are useful mainly as decorations for cocktail tables. We shall pass over these in silence, though not necessarily in disapproval: there are worse things to put on cocktail tables.

Among the good ones is Helmut Breve and Gottfried Gruben's *Greek Temples, Theaters, and Shrines,* which, although not infallible, and possibly overproduced, is still worth the $30.00 it costs. It is full of good information and good pictures.

An excellent and well illustrated account of sculpture is *Greek Sculpture* by Reinhard Lullies ($17.50).

Another big, lavish, and excellent book is *Crete and Mycenae* by Spyridon Marinatos ($25.00).

All three of these volumes have excellent photographs by Max Hirmer and are published by Harry N. Abrams.

A first-rate book for a small fraction of the cost of the ones just mentioned is *Greek Painting* by Pierre Devambez (Viking, $2.25).

Probably the best book on its subject, more detailed and more reliable than Breve and Gruben, but not so handsome, is William Bell Dinsmoor's *The Architecture of Ancient Greece,* of which a new edition is in preparation.

Well illustrated and a bargain is Friedrich Matz's *The Art of Crete and Early Greece* (Crown, $6.95). The translation, however, seems to have been managed rather casually, with the result that a generally fascinating (though technical) text is occasionally impenetrable. One reads, for example, that "the Hittites were unable to make any headway against the strong pressure for massive compositions." Fancy that.

Finally, while you travel through Greece, you may want to pick up the various volumes in the locally-produced series entitled "The Face of Greece." They cost $1.20 or $1.50 apiece, which works out to about a penny a picture.

FOR FUN

Many of the books we recommend require pretty close attention. A great deal can be picked up from the following books even while you are pleasantly relaxing:

Mary Renault's *The King Must Die* (Pocket Books, 75¢) is a plausible and absorbing reconstruction of the Minoan-Mycenaean civilization, though her Theseus sometimes seems like the hero of an adult Western. The sequel, *The Bull from the Sea* (Pocket Books, 75¢) is perhaps a little much of a good thing and shows the strain of rationalizing the old stories. Her earlier book, *The Last of the Wine* (Pocket Books, 75¢), gives an idea of life at the time of the Peloponnesian War.

There are two good mysteries based on the horrible civil war of 1945-9, when many more Greeks were killed—most of them in cold blood—than in all the battles, air raids, and German reprisals (which were sufficently horrible) of World War II. For some reason, this war was not thought important by the American press; so it may come as a surprise—and certainly as a shock—to you to learn that many thousand Greeks, most of them children, were kidnapped, and some are still held, as hostages in Bulgaria and Albania; and that at one point the Communists controlled most of Athens, hit the Parthenon thirty-two times with mortar fire, and displayed the corpses of their opponents by the hundreds in Constitution Square. All these things happened and form the chilling background for Helen MacInnes's *Decision at Delphi* (Crest, 60¢) and Mary Stewart's *My Brother Michael* (Crest, 50¢).

Then there is a numerous class of informal travel books. By all odds the wittiest and most informative is Osbert Lancaster's *Classical Landscape with Figures,* unfortunately out of print in the United States. But your bookseller can get it for you from England (John Murray, publisher) if you allow a month or so for the transaction, or you can pick up a copy in Athens. It is highly recommended for reading after your trip is over.

If you are tempted by the "island extras" of our Chapter 15, there are two books you will find interesting. Both are personal. The first is Ernle Bradford's *The Companion Guide to the Greek Islands* (Harper & Row, $4.95). More personal, and more interesting, is Robert Payne's *The Isles of Greece* (Simon & Schuster, $7.50).

Christopher Rand's *Grecian Calendar* had a considerable vogue when it was first published. We found it misleading for travelers who did not have all year—as Rand did—to savor Greece. If a place requires a couple of weeks to appreciate (as some places do), there is no sense trying to make anything of it in a couple of hours.

Eric and Aileen Forbes-Boyd's *In Crusader Greece* (Norton, $5.50) is a delightful introduction to a side of Greece we have scarcely touched on.

Henry Miller's *The Colossus of Maroussi* (New Directions, $1.35) is an engaging sport, not like other Miller effusions, but more like Thoreau with a Brooklyn accent.

Lawrence Durrell's *Reflections on a Marine Venus* (Dutton, $1.75) is perhaps more notable for the fact that

Durrell wrote it than for what it has to say about Rhodes. The volume also contains *Prospero's Cell,* which is about Corfu.

The novels of Kazantzakis are all worth reading, as are two novels by Americans: Glenway Wescott's moving *Apartment in Athens* (about the German occupation) and May Sarton's *Joanna and Ulysses* (about its aftermath).

Having saturated yourself with Greece and the Greeks, you may turn with profit to Herbert J. Muller's *The Loom of History* (Oxford, $2.95; New American Library, 95¢), an assessment of the Hellenic contribution to civilization in comparison with that of other ancients. Muller's thoughtful book should stimulate you to explore pastures new.

TWO PAMPHLETS FOR FLOWER LOVERS

"Greece," says A. J. Huxley, "has a flora of at least 6,000 species. . . . About one plant in ten is endemic—one found nowhere else." We ourselves casually counted over fifty different kinds of flowers beside the path of one hillside in Karytena.

There is no readily accessible book on the subject, but there are two pamphlets worth writing for. One, from which we quote, is called *Flowers in Greece: An Outline of the Flora* and is published by the Royal Horticultural Society, Vincent Square, London, S. W. 1. It runs to 44 pages, has 23 color plates and a map, and costs three shillings sixpence (50¢), plus another shilling or two for postage.

The other, entitled *Garden Lore of Athens,* is published by the American School of Classical Studies in Athens, % Institute for Advanced Study, Princeton, N.J. It has 51 illustrations, 10 of them in color, and sells for $1.00, postpaid.

APPENDIX 3

A FEW NOTES
FOR CAMERA ADDICTS

> For Praxiteles, indeed even for Alcamenes,
> the image of a god is not an object to be
> approached by the artist with reverence,
> but an occasion for the solving of an artis-
> tic problem.
>
> MARTIN P. NILSSON, A History
> of Greek Religion

Every book you have ever read on Greece talks of the
crystal purity of the air, the transparent blue of the sky,
and so on. There is truth in this, but let us say that there
used to be more than there is now. Athens, in particular,
has all the natural, industrial, and automotive advantages
required to produce smog to rival Los Angeles in intensity, if not extensiveness. One can seldom any longer
get a clear view of Phaleron or Piraeus from the Acropolis;
and what one sees as one looks out from Lykabettos tends
to be softened by an all-pervading haze. Not that it is
not lovely in spite of all.

You will, therefore, have more need of a haze filter
than of an intensity filter, unless you plan to experiment
with Ektachrome. Friends of ours have successfully used
Ektachrome, without an intensity filter in museums and
with a filter outdoors, but we, with less confidence in
ourselves, have stuck to Kodachrome II and have amassed

enough slides to cure insomnia in any neighbors we can induce to sit before our screen.

We have often wished we could do better in museums than we have been able to, because it is seldom possible to buy postcards or commercially prepared slides of all the things one would like to have pictures of. It would do no harm to waste a roll or two perfecting your flash technique at home before you go. You will be asked to check your camera at the entrance of each museum, but for an extra fee, usually 5 drachmas, you can shoot to your heart's content. Tripods, however, are forbidden, which may seem odd in a land that once was the home of the tripod, but is a necessary provision, else one could not make one's way through the forest of them that would spring up in front of the Mask of Agamemnon and all the other great things.

INDEX

A NOTE ABOUT THE AUTHORS

GEORGE BROCKWAY was born in Portland, Maine, in 1915. He was graduated from Williams College in 1936 and later attended Yale Graduate School. He worked for the McGraw-Hill Book Company until 1942, when he went to W. W. Norton & Company, Inc., of which he has been president since 1958. LUCILE BROCKWAY was born in Burlington, Vermont, and was graduated from Smith College in 1939. They made their maiden voyage to Greece in 1963 and have made subsequent trips, including an exploration of the islands on a yacht shared with friends. The Brockways have seven children and their permanent home is in Chappaqua, New York.

A NOTE ON THE TYPE

The text of this book was set on the Linotype in a new face called Primer, designed by Rudolph Ruzicka, earlier responsible for the design of Fairfield and Fairfield Medium, Linotype faces whose virtues have for some time now been accorded wide recognition.

The complete range of sizes of Primer was first made available in 1954, although the pilot size of 12 point was ready as early as 1951. The design of the face makes general reference to Linotype Century (long a serviceable type, totally lacking in manner or frills of any kind) but brilliantly corrects the characterless quality of that face.

The book was designed by Betty Anderson and was composed, printed, and bound by The Haddon Craftsmen, Inc., Scranton, Pennsylvania. The illustrations were printed by Philips Offset, Inc., New York City.